Make Your Move

Make Your Move

For Ambitious People Ready to Live Their Aspirations

Marlon Styles, Jr.

ConnectEDD Publishing
Hanover, Pennsylvania

Copyright © 2025 by Marlon Styles, Jr.

All rights reserved. No part of this publication may be reproduced, distributed, or transmitted in any form or by any means, including photocopying, recording, or other electronic or mechanical methods, without the prior written permission of the publisher, except in the case of brief quotations embodied in critical reviews and certain other noncommercial uses permitted by copyright law. For permission requests, contact the publisher at: info@connecteddpublishing.com

This publication is available at discount pricing when purchased in quantity for educational purposes, promotions, or fundraisers. For inquiries and details, contact the publisher at: info@connecteddpublishing.com

Published by ConnectEDD Publishing LLC
Hanover, PA
www.connecteddpublishing.com

Cover Design: Kheila Casas

Make Your Move — 1st ed. Paperback
ISBN   979-8-9988361-7-6

Praise for *Make Your Move*

Marlon Styles is one of the most ambitious leaders I know, and his passion shines through every page of this book. *Make Your Move* is more than a roadmap; it's a call to action for anyone ready to step boldly into their purpose and create lasting impact. With powerful stories, practical strategies, and an authentic voice, this book challenges you to dream bigger while giving you the tools to make those dreams real. If you're serious about elevating your leadership, your career, or your life, this is the book to read!

—Thomas C. Murray | 2x Best-Selling Author

Marlon Style's *Make Your Move* is a bold and inspiring guide for leaders who want to lead with ambition, courage, and humility. Through powerful storytelling from his own journey, Marlon connects deeply with readers, offering wisdom that is both practical and heartfelt. This book challenges leaders to rise above fear and doubt while reminding them that true leadership is rooted in service. A must-read for anyone ready to step forward with ambition and purpose.

—Glenn Robbins | Award-Winning Educational Leader, Best Selling Author, Speaker

Make Your Move is a powerful guide for anyone who refuses to settle for less than their full potential. With practical principles and motivating wisdom, it equips ambitious people to believe bigger, stay disciplined, and embrace the journey of becoming. This book doesn't just inspire—it provides the roadmap to actually live your aspirations. This truly a must-read for leaders, dreamers, and anyone committed to excellence.

—Martha Salazar Zamora | Superintendent

Make Your Move is a book that speaks directly to the heart of every ambitious person who has ever wrestled with both purpose and ambition. Marlon Styles reminds us that ambition is not about chasing titles but about elevating others, and his stories brought me back to the moments that shaped my own calling to serve students. I found myself nodding often, encouraged by his honesty about setbacks and inspired by his belief that joy and discipline can coexist on the journey forward. This book feels less like advice and more like a conversation with a trusted mentor who wants you to succeed. I am grateful for the reminder that the most ambitious move any of us can make is to live with courage, integrity, and a relentless commitment to others.

   –Jason Van Heukelum | Superintendent

In a world where careers are built on strategy, not luck, *Make Your Move* is the playbook. With sharp insights and proven tools, it equips professionals to navigate transitions with confidence and purpose. This is essential reading for leaders and changemakers alike.

   –Gustavo Balderas | National Superintendent of the Year
     AASA and NABE

Marlon Styles delivers an inspiring call to action for educators and leaders to step forward with courage and purpose. *Make Your Move* blends practical wisdom with visionary leadership, making it a must-read for anyone committed to raising the bar and transforming communities.

   –Dr. Andraé Townsel | Superintendent and CEO of Hartford
     Public Schools; President-Elect, National Alliance of Black
     School Educators

Make Your Move resonated deeply with me. Having experienced both the drive to be my best and the challenges of rejection, I found this book to be a powerful reminder that achievement extends beyond success. It's about resilience, growth, learning, impact, and leading with purpose while remaining authentic. This book is an essential read for both aspiring and experienced leaders, and I look forward to sharing it with my mentors and mentees.

   –Dr. Rosa Perez-Iziah | Assistant Superintendent, Author, Presenter, Consultant

Marlon Styles, Jr. is a passionate author who inspires readers to more deeply understand the meaning and drivers of ambition. *Make Your Move* is a motivating guide for ambitious people in any industry, providing actionable strategies to align their ambitions with their core values to make a meaningful and lasting impact on those around them.

   –Keith D. Bricking, MD | Chief Clinical Officer, Executive Vice President Premier Health

As someone who has navigated multiple career transitions within education, I know that ambition without strategy is just wishful thinking. Marlon Styles provides the practical framework ambitious people need to position themselves for meaningful opportunities. What sets this book apart is its honest examination of the gap between preparing for an opportunity and thriving once you get there. Styles doesn't just motivate, he shows you how to build the belief systems and disciplined habits that make success sustainable. His emphasis on letting your work speak for itself rather than chasing external validation resonates deeply with anyone who understands the difference between performance and true impact. This is essential reading for anyone ready to move beyond hoping for their next opportunity to strategically earning it.

   –Lynette White Founder | CEO Lynette White Social, LLC Author of the Ed Branding Book

Dedication

For Rudolph Watson–My grandfather. I spent my childhood watching you lead with strength, speak with kindness, and serve others without ever asking for anything in return. I wanted to be just like you when I grew up. I still do. You're no longer here, but your voice, your walk, and your spirit guide me every day. I miss you more than words can carry.

Table of Contents

Introduction: *Why Move with Ambition?* 1
    Your Journey: The Starting Point. 10
    Move with Ambition 17

Chapter 1: *Core Principles of Ambitious Movement* 23
    What Does it Mean to "Move with Ambition"? 23
    What Moving with Ambition Looks Like 28
    The Definition That Moves Us Forward. 29
    The Four Key Principles: Purpose, Vision, Bold Agency,
        and Disciplined Consistency 30
    Position Yourself for Success: Taking Intentional Steps
        Toward Ambitious Growth 43
    Understand What Sets You Apart. 43
    Be Selective About Opportunities 44
    Develop Depth, Not Just Breadth 45
    Strengthen Your Personal Brand 47
    Foster a Proactive Mindset 48
    Create a Network of Encouragers 49
    Anticipate What's Next. 51

Chapter 2: *Permission to Believe* 55
    Coming Together with Your Belief 55
    Blueprint Box Activities. 57
    Building Self-Awareness 60

Committing to What You Believe 63
Building Your Personal Belief Structure 64
Strengthening Your Belief Daily........................... 67

Chapter 3: *Harness the Power of Discipline* 71
Realities of Your Behaviors 71
Momentum Markers 75
Mapping Your Momentum Markers: A Strategic
  Experience 76

Chapter 4: *Navigating the Ambitious Journey* 89
The Ambitious Move..................................... 89
What Brings You Joy? 97
Turning Setbacks Into Comebacks 100

Chapter 5: *Let Your Work Speak for Itself* 103
The Weight of Expectation and the Work That Endures..... 103
Strategic Integrity Over External Optics 106
Personal Philosophy of Execution 108
Ready Now 100: Planting Seeds for Future Impact 112
Call to Action and Reflection Prompts 118

Chapter 6: *Stepping Into the Right Fit* 121
Lesson 1: Same Purpose—A Shift in the Path Forward 123
Lesson 2: Reality Check—A Desire for a Better Fit.......... 126
Lesson 3: Thriving—The Opportunity Fit My Purpose 129
Stretch Prompt: Identity and Opportunity Map............ 132
How the Lessons Connect with Your Journey Thus Far...... 132
Bridging Reflection to Decision 134
Opportunity Alignment Assessment Tool: Is This the
  Right Fit? 134
Closing the Chapter: Make Your Move..................... 142

TABLE OF CONTENTS

Chapter 7: *Living the Move* 143
    Interview: Kenny Glenn–"Remain Courageous" 147
    Interview: Kristen Brooks–"Who I'm Becoming" 149
    Interview: Kristine Gilmore–"Living In Purpose-Driven Work" 151
    Interview: Antonio Shelton–"A Unified Team Living the Move" 153
    Reflection: Living in the Move 157
    Reflection Activity: Who Are You Becoming? 157

Conclusion: *Make Your Move* 159

References 169

Acknowledgements 171

About the Author 173

More from ConnectEDD Publishing 175

Ambitious Person:

Someone who sees an end worth pursuing and dares to believe they can reach it.

INTRODUCTION

Why Move with Ambition?

Every educator has a moment. A moment that reminds you why you chose this path and why you continue, even when the challenges feel overwhelming. It's a moment that changes everything—not just for your students, but for you. For some, it's the breakthrough of a student who finally believes in themselves. For others, it's the realization that your words, actions, and belief in someone else has a real influence far beyond what you can see. It's the moment that ignites something inside you—a drive to do more, to be more, to move with ambition and purpose.

Take a moment to think about something. By name, who was the one person who made you fall in love with what you do or want to do? For me, I had a student named Tanner. See, I'm an old-school middle school math teacher at heart, and loved everything about working with young people. In 2005, I was teaching 8th grade math on *Team Ambition* at Pleasant Run Middle School. I was lucky enough to be teamed up with Julie Flack, Tiffany Mosley, and Megan Poneris. It was my fourth year of teaching and it turned out to be one of my favorite school years as an educator—all because of a student named Tanner.

I met Tanner at the start of his 8th-grade year and immediately took note of how intelligent, mature, confident, and passionate he was. In the spirit of the story, I have to kick it off by saying if Tanner were writing this story, he'd probably start by saying he hated being in 8th grade math class with Mr. Styles. Room 99, my math classroom, was alive with energy. I even had a boom box playing music while we "learned" math. Yes, a boom box—the kind that takes six D batteries. My students loved it, and I rolled with it. My students and I started the year off trying to relate to each other. I tried talking to all my students, including Tanner, about things I thought they were interested in. Pouring into my students was something I prided myself on. I wanted nothing more than to have such a positive influence that every student discovered their best selves and felt like they were the most important person in the world. As I was doing this, I should have been paying attention to the impact Tanner was having on me.

We started the first few months bumping heads while trying to figure out how to connect with one another. I found myself trying my best not to give Tanner behavior points in his team planner. A few months into the school year, I noticed that when Tanner became frustrated with the math, he would let out a loud "Ah man!" I immediately became frustrated, too, because it "disrupted" the class. I quickly realized that when I heard "Ah man!" it meant that Tanner needed me to swing by his desk to simply check in. Over time, Tanner accumulated a number of points in his planner and it warranted some consequences. This trend continued throughout the second quarter, and I found myself thinking about why Tanner couldn't figure out how to function in my class. Thinking I was helping Tanner mature, I doubled down on trying to help Tanner be more aware of his behaviors in class. I admit this was the moment I really started to really care about his success. When he received his first out of school suspension, it hit me hard.

Pleasant Run Middle School sits at the bottom of a hill across from a cemetery off Pippin Road. I found myself sitting in my car one day after school crying as a grown man because Tanner kept getting in trouble. I wanted the kid to be so successful that it started to significantly impact me. I sat in the car asking myself, "What can I do as a teacher so this kid can feel welcomed in my class and enjoy some success?" For the first time, I was taking ownership of my classroom environment and how it was impacting Tanner. I had to make a change so that things could change for Tanner, and it worked. In the second semester, we started to click and it felt fantastic. Tanner smiled and laughed more often in class, and he was enjoying some success academically. By the end of the year, Tanner was thriving. I'll always remember our project-based learning unit on Systems of Equations, where we created a T-shirt business. Watching him and his classmates succeed was incredibly rewarding. Our relationship had grown stronger. Tanner didn't need me to be a disciplinarian in 8th grade. Tanner needed me to believe in him and hold him accountable for being his best self. On the last day of school, I was proud to see my 8th graders move on to 9th grade at Northwest High School.

That summer, Principal Reynolds from Northwest High School offered me an Assistant Principal position. This was the high school where all my 8th grade students would start their high school careers. I was thrilled to accept the position and even more excited to learn I'd be overseeing the 9th grade class. If Tanner were writing this story, he'd probably start by saying he hated being in 9th grade at Northwest High School with Mr. Styles, but it was my goal to make sure Tanner got off to a great start to his high school experience. My new role as assistant principal did not allow for the daily interactions I'd cherished as a teacher, but I made it a priority to stay connected to Tanner by visiting him in his Algebra class. That year, I worked closely with his parents to support him, but unfortunately, Tanner's 9th grade year was marked by disciplinary challenges that often landed him in my office. When he came down to my office, his head would hang really low as if he were disappointed in himself. We engaged in several conversations early that year as I worked to pour into the young man. His parents were supportive and believed in him. Issuing discipline to Tanner was one of the hardest things I've ever done. I wanted so badly to see him succeed. I tried my best to speak with his teacher about different ways to connect with him. One day, the principal told me, "It's time." With a very confused look on my face, I responded with, "What do you mean, 'It's time.'?" Not sure about you, but I was thinking I don't have time for lunch and I don't have time to get all my voicemails answered. Unfortunately, "It's time" meant something different., Tanner's behavior had escalated to the point where an expulsion was the topic. He told me it was time to issue the consequence.

I'll never forget the day I had to issue Tanner's expulsion. It was the worst day I ever had as an educator. Tanner—this intelligent, strong, passionate young man—was sitting across from me as I delivered the news. It is hard to even think about that day. Driving home that day, I couldn't hold back my emotions. I thought about the bright future I saw in him and how heartbroken I was by the situation.

By name, Tanner is the student who made me fall in love with education. He taught me the importance of celebrating what students bring to us every day. I fell in love with my responsibility to work with students, inspiring them to embrace their dreams in life, supporting them in their journey, and being there for them when they needed a life changer. In my role as a Principal, Executive Director for Curriculum & Instruction, Superintendent, and now Consultant, I have taken pride in staying true to my promise to inspire as many Tanners as possible through my work.

WHY MOVE WITH AMBITION?

Following the expulsion, I lost touch with Tanner for almost twenty years, but thought of him often. In November 2023, I received a message from him on Facebook. This was the letter from Tanner that brought me to tears of joy:

> *Man, it brings me so much joy to see you still so passionate about teaching! I certainly wasn't an exemplary student, didn't pick up everything I should've regarding math, history, etc., and certainly put way too much effort into being the cool kid. But I think I picked up something far more valuable from you.*
>
> *My 8th grade year—do you remember? I got suspended five times in the first quarter, one more and I was gone for good. I don't remember a specific conversation or anything, but I remember you being on my and pushing me constantly after that. We butted heads at first, but I came to respect you so much because you never gave up on me, you always kept it real with me! I needed the tough love.*
>
> *I'd love to say things were all great after that. Maybe you know, maybe not, but after getting kicked out of Northwest and graduating ECOT, it was really dark times from age 18-22, as I burned every bridge. However, other people like you entered my life and showed me that I was capable of being the man I wanted to be. I've been sober for the last ten years, have a wife and three beautiful daughters, and own a successful business in Florida building six-figure swimming pools and employing several others.*
>
> *I say all this to say, there's a good chance I wouldn't be where I am today if it wasn't for people like you investing in me. Please keep that passion that drives you to pour yourself into our youth, and know that what you do changes lives—you certainly did mine!*
>
> *I wish you the best, Mr. Styles.*

Wow! This letter touched my soul in ways that words cannot explain. I poured everything I had into Tanner because I believed in him. Little did the young man know that the impact he was having on me fueled my love for the profession.

In the spirit of this story, it ends with one of the most inspiring moments of my career. Not long after receiving Tanner's message, I found myself driving down a highway in Florida on my way to meet Tanner at a café. We sat and talked for hours on a Saturday morning. He was still the same Tanner—intelligent, confident, full of passion, and proud of the life he'd built. He challenged me to share our story to inspire other educators to connect with their students in meaningful ways. That day, I made a promise to Tanner: I would share our story. I made a promise to myself to be better, to do more, and be a person who inspires others. It has become one of my greatest ambitions to inspire educators across the country to see the power of their relationships and the impact they can have on students like Tanner. Tanner is the one student who made me fall in love with serving as an educator. Although there are many, three other students inspired my love for being in education and I want to say their names: Christian Bonner, Dorthy Tatum, and Samu'El Fowler. There is a story behind each of those names. At the core of them? They fueled my love for education.

By name, who was the student who made you fall in love with being an educator? If you are not an educator, who was the person that made you fall in love with what you do or aspire to do? Welcome the emotions that surface as you reflect on the interactions and moments of the relationship. Share that story with others. Share that story with the student or that person. The love you have for what you do will be a key source of inspiration for your next ambitious move. Let it be your call to action.

Here's the truth: education is filled with moments when opportunity and adversity mix beautifully. For every Tanner, there's another student whose potential is waiting to be unlocked. For every Tanner, there's an educator standing at a crossroads, deciding

WHY MOVE WITH AMBITION?

whether to lean in or hold back. Maybe you're at that crossroads right now. Maybe you're feeling the pull to do more, to lead in new ways, or to take the next step in your career. Maybe you've started dreaming about what's possible—what it would look like to advance your career or elevate your capacity to make an even greater impact. Maybe, you applied or expressed interest in a new opportunity, and didn't get selected. Now it's time to use that resilience as a foundation for something extraordinary. Before you move forward, it's essential to reconnect with the reason you started. Reconnecting to your purpose is the first step in reigniting your ambition. It's about looking back on the moments that defined you—not to dwell on them, but to use them as fuel for what's next. It's about remembering that every challenge is an opportunity to grow, to dream bigger, and to move with confidence and courage.

Every day you are promised two things. We all get the same two things as we move through the joys of working in the career fields of our choice. When we enter the doors of the workplace, we are greeted each day with a choice and a chance. We find ourselves face to face with moments in our careers where adversity introduces itself into our journey, and it impacts our hearts and our minds. Adversity, I've learned, isn't something to fear. It's an invitation. It invites us to reflect, to rediscover our strengths, and to ask ourselves hard questions:

> When we enter the doors of the workplace, we are greeted each day with a choice and a chance.

What am I truly capable of?
How can I create the most impact?

Opportunity, on the other hand, is what emerges when we answer those questions with action. Together, they create the perfect conditions for transformation—both for us and for those we serve. In my role as a classroom teacher, district leader, and superintendent, I have embraced a journey fueled by purpose and driven by a clear sense of direction. Just like you, I approach each day with intention, a motivation to bring my aspirations to life, and a willingness to accept the productive struggle knowing it won't deter my progress. This joyful journey is not just about chasing success, it's about cultivating a mindset that seeks growth, embraces challenges, and aims to make a lasting impact on the people I serve. I have learned to move with ambition.

Back in 1998, I took the Praxis Test in an attempt to acquire my teaching license in the state of Ohio. The required score for Test Code: 0523 (Principles of Learning & Teaching 5-9) was a 168. When my results came back, I discovered my score was two points shy of passing the test. I went on to take that test two more times only to continue scoring a 166. For the first time in my professional journey, I was faced with adversity. Frustrations surfaced, and emotions negatively impacted my ambitious aspirations. Four years into the profession, I applied for a leadership role in Wyoming City Schools. I remember going to the mailbox one day only to find a piece of mail from Wyoming City Schools informing me that I would not be considered for the position. It immediately felt like I had been punched in the gut. Once again, I found myself trying to deal with self-doubt as a result of things not going my way. With that being said, I have been lucky to work with some amazing educators in my career and experience varying degrees of success. Similar to you, I have endured events in my career and life that have provided me with opportunities to grow and mature. Events that made me revisit my passions, goals, and aspirations only to question myself. Not sure about you, but I have certainly challenged myself to answer the question, "Are you cut out for this? Do you have what it takes?" I have even reached out to mentors and people I trusted for guidance and advice. The presence of a mindset not capable of handling negative outcomes, absolutely impacted my ability to make aspirational choices and take advantage of chances to contribute to my school. Luckily, I was able to push through these events and become a better servant leader that people could count on. These experiences early on in my career led me to a professional promise that I have made to others to always find a way to support them. It is time to fulfill that promise, and try to pay it forward to other professionals. There is a mantra that I have tried to live by as someone who cares about the success of others:

> *It's not about what you do for others.*
> *It's about what you put into others.*

You may ask what fills my cup? What brings me joy? Being trusted by fellow educators, colleagues, leaders, or friends to help them find clarity in their life's journey or professional career. These interactions start with conversations about the person having a passion to make a move that will impact their current situation in a positive way. At the core of every conversation with someone, I always discover a sense of ambition and aspiration. Over the years, I have engaged with people who have aspirations of becoming an instructional coach, school psychologist, leader, Superintendent, or just being better at serving children. We have participated in some authentic, intense, and emotional conversations around what they want to do next to positively impact their current reality. Countless interactions have taken place over early morning breakfasts, conversations during a teacher's plan period, Saturday morning phone calls, and conferences. I have learned to ask questions based on curiosity with positive intentions behind them. Most importantly,

I have worked to gain the trust of others to ensure we have a high level of comfort so honest professional dialogue is ensured for the benefit of the person seeking support. Having followed their journeys, celebrated the evolution of their mindset, and reflected on a number of conversations, I have come to believe that when you are motivated by your aspirations and intentionally move with ambition, success is highly probable. The most transformational journeys I have witnessed, all consisted of similar components:

1. Presence of an Ambitious Mindset
2. Understanding How to Position Oneself to Be Successful
3. Ability to Adapt to Change and Overcome Obstacles
4. Consistency in Routine
5. A Joyful Spirit that is Confident and Courageous

I shared with a friend of mine that I was taking the challenge to do something that was hard for me. To write a book. When they asked what I was going to write about, I told them a book about moving through life with ambition. Offering readers advice on how to strategically put yourself in the best possible position to achieve your goals. Their response was, "That sounds just like you." The purpose of this book is to offer ambitious people, who are curious about what they are capable of, a reference to elevate their efforts to experience joyful ambition.

Your Journey: The Starting Point

Ambition may ignite in a single moment, but the path forward begins with the work of reconnecting to your story and purpose. That initial spark must translate into intentional preparation-the starting point of any meaningful journey. But clarity alone isn't enough—it must lead to action. Defining ambition gives you a vision of what is possible, but taking that first step requires reconnecting with the reason you began this journey in the first place. It's time to revisit your story, to reflect on the moments that shaped your purpose and reignited your passion. Your story is your anchor, and as you prepare to move forward, it will serve as both your compass and your fuel.

> Your story is your anchor, and as you prepare to move forward, it will serve as both your compass and your fuel.

Every educator has a story, a series of moments that define why they do what they do. These stories are often intertwined with the lives of people or students—those who challenge us, inspire us, and remind us of the profound impact of our work. Think back to your own "Tanner moment." Who was the student or individual who reminded you of your purpose and reignited your love for this profession? That moment was not accidental; it was a turning point that called you to action. For me, these moments are reminders that our work in education goes far beyond the day-to-day routines. They're opportunities to reflect, reset, and realign with what matters most. They're a reminder of why we chose this profession in the first place.

Your story holds power because it reflects both your journey and your potential. It captures the lessons learned through adversity, the joy of seeing others succeed, and the quiet moments when everything clicks, and you remember why you started. As you reconnect with your story, allow yourself to relive the emotions and lessons that came with it. Let those memories remind you of the influence you have and the possibilities ahead. This is where ambition begins—not with a goal, but with a purpose rooted in your lived experiences.

Mr. Farmer was a teacher I looked up to as a high school student. He was a teacher, coach, and a mentor who always made time for me to talk about how to get where you wanted to go in life. In 2006 when I entered administration as a high school assistant principal, Mr. Farmer was a district administrator. Luckily for me, I had the opportunity to watch one of my favorite educators showcase what successful leadership looked like. The entire district respected him as a leader, his work had an impact on the entire system, he cared about the direction of the district, and always focused on the people. He set a standard that I tried to live up to as a very new leader.

During my second year as an assistant principal, I found myself on committees led by Mr. Farmer. Just like in high school, I made sure to take advantage of every interaction with him. We held several conversations about leadership, serving others, and my career. I share this background because, like so many educators, I found myself with a desire for something different professionally. My ambition was to become a principal who changed the way students experienced school, and to do my part to help educators fall in love with being in education.

I specifically remember a conversation with Mr. Farmer in his office. A few weeks prior, I sent him an email asking to talk about my interest in serving as a principal. The very next morning, I woke up to an email from Mr. Farmer with a date and time to connect. The days leading up to the meeting I found myself getting nervous about telling the person I had looked up to for so long that my dream was to be like him. I wrote down three bulleted topics to cover in the conversation with one of them being a question that would change my entire career. Not knowing it at the time, but this was the moment I learned the importance of the starting point of every journey. As I was chasing this dream of becoming a principal, I found myself questioning my readiness and entered this conversation thinking about experiences to prepare me. Deep into the conversation, I reached the third bullet, and I asked Mr. Farmer, "How do you know when you are ready?" Like always, in his calm and methodical demeanor, he replied with a single statement.

He said, "You will never be ready, but you can begin preparing for the big move."

Prepare! All I could think about was getting myself prepared. So, I went back to the office and went to work. I set new mindsets and habits purely focused on key areas to prepare myself for future big professional moves. To be clear, this was not about gaining access to different experiences. At the time I needed to elevate my ability to communicate clearly, to partner with someone to accomplish shared goals, think about the big picture, and to develop consistency in how I led. My responsibilities that year were to lead the Special Education Department and Social Studies Department at Northwest High School. I decided to use these leadership areas as the starting point in my journey to begin preparing for the ambitious move I wanted to make. My partnerships with the department chairs, Mrs. Humbert and Mrs. Disbro, were the preparation investments that changed my ability to pursue my ambitions. These two amazing leaders offered a genuine professional relationship that centered on a common purpose: to positively impact the culture of the school. They taught me how to communicate, the importance of working alongside others, caring about the capacity of the team, and executing a co-created plan for improvement. Together we handled adversity, celebrated progress, and were always there for one another. These are three things that I take great pride in doing in the present day fourteen years later. Mrs. Humbert and Mrs. Disbro challenged me to follow through on my commitment to lead, to spark self-growth, and to shift my mindset to prepare myself for being the leader I wanted to be. Mrs. Humbert and Mrs. Disbro became vital components in my ability to prepare for the ambitious move that I wanted to make. I am forever grateful for their investment in my preparation. Why is this short story so important? It introduces the importance of the starting point of every journey we have as ambitious people.

During the Summer of 2024, I received a call from an educator friend after they applied for an assistant principal job opening. I have a great deal of respect and admiration for this aspiring leader, and know for a fact they would add value to any school community. The educator had finished the interview process, and found out they were not selected. The call became emotional when frustration surfaced about "Why I wasn't picked." I responded by asking, "What did you do to prepare for the opportunity?" The educator talked about the committees they served on, the extra duties they took on, and other internship type experiences they felt made them prepared for the opportunity. I was guilty of this same mindset early in my career: thinking the list of experiences would be the way I showed an interview team that I was the right person for the job. But did these experiences really prepare this aspirational leader? Or were they just a series of experiences? In this situation, the decision on who was the best candidate for the job was not based on the list of experiences on the resume. The decision was based on the candidate who had the best set of skills, abilities, beliefs, and educational practices for the job.

We all deal with varying degrees of emotions on this journey. Rejection is when you might not be chosen for an opportunity, position, or recognition you desired or worked toward. It offers a sign that your effort, skill, or presence did not align with the needs, preferences, or standards of the deciding body. Rejection can often bring disappointment, self-doubt, sadness, frustration, or even shame. It may lead to you questioning your ability, value, or loyalty especially when you tie your self-worth to the outcome. Mindset matters in how you receive any type of rejection. Know that rejection can spark self-reflection and resilience, offering motivation to try it again or seek a new path. A different emotion comes when the journey ends with the desired outcome of being selected or earning the new role. When this happens it is an affirmation, alignment, and validation of your efforts, qualities, and fit. It brings a stronger sense of pride, joy, confidence, and sense of accomplishment. You will more than likely feel a sense of belonging and purpose. Be aware of the additional weight of expectations and the internal motivation to live up to the choice. Both rejection and being selected offer lessons. The key is how you process each of these as either finite outcomes or part of your larger journey toward fulfillment.

Just like Mr. Farmer, I want to emphasize the importance of making an early commitment to prepare yourself as you start and go through your journey to live your aspirations. Challenge yourself to clearly define your ambitions, establish your commitment, and work to identify a target list of preparations you need to make to move with ambition.

Before you kick off your journey, let's take some time to consider two mindset approaches that people often assume as they enter the start of their effort to move with ambition: An aspirational mindset and a mindset of feeling unready. Let's frame both mindsets:

- **Aspirational Mindset**
  What It Is: A mindset rooted in optimism, belief in personal growth, and the drive to pursue goals despite uncertainties or limitations.
  How It Works:
  + Focuses on possibilities and opportunities rather than obstacles.
  + Embraces challenges as part of the journey toward growth and success.

- Views "not being ready" as a temporary state that can be overcome through preparation, learning, and action.
- Sees setbacks as lessons, not endpoints.

How It Feels:
- Empowering and motivating.
- Encourages risk-taking and innovation.
- Builds confidence and resilience over time.

- **Mindset of Feeling Unready**

  What It Is: A mindset influenced by self-doubt, fear of failure, or a belief that current abilities or circumstances are insufficient to take on challenges.

  How It Works:
  - Focuses on what is lacking instead of what is possible.
  - Amplifies fear of rejection, judgment, or failure.
  - May delay action until "perfect" conditions or full readiness are achieved (which may never come).
  - Interprets setbacks as evidence of inadequacy.
  - Sees setbacks as endpoints, not lessons.

  How It Feels:
  - Limiting and discouraging.
  - Creates anxiety, frustration, or paralysis.
  - Can erode confidence over time and prevent meaningful progress.

Perspective on Competing Mindsets

Mindset	Aspirational	Feeling Unready
Focus	Growth, Opportunities, Possibilities	Limitations, Fears, Inadequacies
Approach	Starts Before Being Fully Ready, and Learns on the Go	Waits for Until Feeling Perfectly Ready
Response to Failure	Learns and Adapts	Interprets as Proof of Inadequacy
Driving Belief	"I'll Figure It Out."	"I'm Not Ready Yet."
Outcome	Builds Confidence and Momentum	Stalls Progress and Fosters Self-Doubt

What is your current mindset? What parts of your story have influenced this mindset? As you enter the starting point of a journey to live your ambitions, what mindset would you like to possess? What are the reasons and how will it impact your ability to actualize what it is you want?

Move with Ambition

To move with ambition is to bring your best self to every opportunity, fully committed to making meaningful contributions. It's about staying laser-focused on the bigger picture while making intentional strides forward. This approach creates a powerful energy that not only propels you, but also inspires those around you. When "Moving with Ambition" is your guide, every choice and action become an opportunity to grow, learn, and achieve. It's a dedication to excellence and resilience that turns dreams into tangible outcomes, not just for yourself but for everyone touched by your journey. Moving with ambition transforms effort into impact and vision into reality, ultimately shaping a path that leaves a positive, lasting legacy.

Each day presents a choice and a chance to make an impact. But I know some days, the choices don't feel as clear, and the chances seem out of reach. Maybe you've been told "no" before. Maybe you've worked tirelessly for an opportunity, poured your heart into preparing for it, only to find out it went to someone else. Maybe you've felt the sting of rejection so deeply that it made you question everything—your abilities, your purpose, and whether you're even on the right path.

I've been there. I know what it feels like to wonder if all the effort is worth it, to ask yourself if you'll ever get your shot. Rejection can feel like the final word, like a door slammed shut on your dreams. But let me tell you something: rejection doesn't define you. It's not the end of the story—it's a moment in the journey, and it's one you can use to grow stronger, sharper, and more determined.

But ambition doesn't always feel like forward momentum. For some of us, it feels stalled—like waiting at the edge of an opportunity that hasn't arrived or chasing a dream that seems just out of reach. Maybe you've felt the ache of working toward a goal only to be told "no" when you were sure you were ready. Maybe you've poured your heart into your work, hoping it would lead to your next big step, only to feel like your efforts have gone unnoticed. Those moments are heavy, and they can make you question everything: *Am I good enough? Did I do something wrong? Should I just stop trying?*

I remember sitting across from an aspiring leader who shared these very questions with me. They had applied for a position that represented everything they'd been working toward for years. When the offer went to someone else, the disappointment was crushing.

WHY MOVE WITH AMBITION?

As we talked, they opened up about the thoughts running through their head: *What could I have done differently? What if this was my only chance? What if I'm not meant to lead?* Their words were laced with self-doubt, and their pain was palpable. I could see the weight they were carrying—the weight of rejection, of uncertainty, of wondering if all the effort had been for nothing.

I told them something I've come to believe deeply: rejection isn't the end of your story. It's a chapter, a moment that holds within it an opportunity to reflect, recalibrate, and grow. It doesn't feel like that in the moment—I know that. Rejection stings because it's personal. It makes us feel as though we've failed, but what if it's not about failure? What if it's about preparing you for what's next?

The aspiring leader sitting across from me wasn't lacking ambition or effort. They weren't lacking potential, either. What they lacked was a clear sense of what they needed to grow. I encouraged them to think about how this moment could prepare them for the next opportunity—not by dwelling on what they didn't achieve, but by identifying what they needed to build. Rejection isn't a verdict; it's an invitation to strengthen the foundation for your next move.

I know some of you reading this are processing aspirations and some are tackling the aftermath of rejection. You've dreamed of a role, a career shift, or a bigger opportunity to make an impact, only to feel like the door hasn't opened wide enough for you to step through it. You're not alone. These moments are part of the journey, and they don't define your worth. They are the moments that challenge you to dig deeper, to reconnect with your purpose, and to prepare in ways you might not have considered before.

This book is here to remind you that you are capable of more than you think. It's here to guide you as you take the next steps toward the goals and dreams that are waiting for you. Whether you're an aspiring educator, a professional preparing for a new role, or someone thinking about your next big move, this book is your resource for growth, reflection, and preparation. It's about moving forward with intention, knowing that every challenge, every setback, and every step along the way is part of what makes you stronger.

> NOTE: For additional, free Make Your Move resources, visit www.marlonstyles/resources

The move you're about to make is not solely about being successful. It's about living in your passion, serving a greater good, and leveraging your unique skills and gifts. Along the way, you'll cultivate what I call "joyful ambition." Joyful ambition is a purpose-driven energy that transforms challenges into growth, grounds you in your values, and brings fulfillment to the work you do. It's about finding joy not just in reaching the destination but in the process of striving toward your goals. This book is designed to help you harness joyful ambition by elevating your behaviors and mindset to turn aspirations into reality.

Each chapter serves as a roadmap, guiding you through the foundations of ambition. Together, we'll explore what it means to set bold aspirations, make meaningful commitments, and overcome the obstacles that inevitably arise. You'll uncover strategies for cultivating consistency, adapting to change, and staying true to your vision. Along the way, we'll focus on the importance of joy and gratitude, helping you find fulfillment in the work you do every day. Beyond personal growth, this book emphasizes the ripple effect of ambition, showing how your actions can inspire and empower others. Ambition, when shared, becomes contagious, creating a legacy that extends far beyond your individual journey.

Understanding our focus is much more than personal achievement. This book is about the legacy of impact that comes from purposeful, resilient actions. It challenges you to define your own

WHY MOVE WITH AMBITION?

"ambitious moment" and take decisive steps toward your vision. It reminds you that true success is found not just in individual growth but in the contributions you make to others. As ambitious people, we have a unique responsibility to create life-changing opportunities for those we serve. At the end of the day, they are relying on us to be our best, to show up for them, and to create the conditions that allow them to thrive. People are counting on you to make your move.

As you read this book, please know that you are capable of far more than you think. I encourage you to approach the journey ahead with peace of mind, confidence in your abilities, and an openness to growth. Let's begin with command of our emotions and a mindset that allows you to experience joy along the way. My hope is that this book challenges the way you think, deepens the way you reflect, and strengthens your belief in your ability to elevate your game. You have everything it takes to succeed, and I'm here to cheer you on every step of the way.

The journey ahead will ask much of you, but it will also give you much in return. With every step, you'll gain clarity, confidence, and the tools to make an even greater impact. Preparation isn't about perfection; it's about progress. It's about making the decision to commit to your ambition, even when the path forward feels uncertain. The work you are about to do will be challenging at times, but it will also be deeply rewarding. It's time to embrace the process, lean into your strengths, and move forward with purpose. As you prepare to dive into this book, understand each chapter is designed to equip you with practical strategies, inspiring stories, and actionable principles to help you move with ambition. This is not just a book to read, but instead a guide to engage with fully, a resource to help you take bold steps toward the future you envision, and use as a catalyst for change. Now, let's get ready to make your move. To make your biggest most ambitious move yet.

CHAPTER 1

Core Principles of Ambitious Movement

What Does It Mean to "Move with Ambition"?

The stories we carry shape our purpose. They remind us of the moments that define us, the people who challenge and inspire us, and the decisions that shape legacies long after the moment has passed. As you reflect on your own journey—your "Tanner" or the experiences that reignited your passion for the profession you chose—you begin to see the threads of ambition woven throughout your story. Ambition is what brings clarity to those moments.

The question now is: How do we turn those defining moments into lasting movement? How do we ensure that our ambition doesn't just sit quietly in the background but drives us forward with intention and purpose? But what does it truly mean to move with ambition? How do we define it, embody it, and channel its transformative power to inspire change within ourselves and the communities we serve?

Before we begin the journey of action, we must ground ourselves in the core of ambition—a concept that is equal parts purpose, passion, and mindset. Ambition is the cornerstone of meaningful and lasting impact, but to truly couple it, we must first understand its power, its purpose, and its potential to shape lives.

Ambition is often misunderstood. It's too often mistaken for a relentless pursuit of personal success—chasing titles, accumulating accolades, or striving for external validation. Others dismiss it as selfish, imagining that ambition focuses only on the individual. But true ambition isn't about status. True ambition is rooted in purpose. It is the deep-seated belief that you are here to make a difference, to elevate others, and to pursue something greater than yourself. Ambition for purpose sees success not as a destination, but as a byproduct of meaningful work.

> True ambition is rooted in purpose. It is the deep-seated belief that you are here to make a difference, to elevate others, and to pursue something greater than yourself.

When was the moment you discovered the difference? Perhaps it was a time when you chose to prioritize the greater good over personal gain. Or maybe it was when you witnessed the ripple effect of your efforts, as someone else's life was changed by your contribution. These moments reveal the truth of ambition—not as a self-centered drive, but as a catalyst for collective impact that inspires action and transforms lives.

Purposeful ambition is the kind that changes cultures and communities. It begins with clarity—knowing why you do what you do and who you serve. We recognize the privilege and responsibility of being a changemaker, educator, or leader. Purposeful ambition not only fuels your goals, it connects them to a larger mission. It drives you to create environments where others can thrive, to challenge systems that hold people back, and to build solutions that inspire hope and opportunity. When ambition is guided by purpose, it becomes a magnetic force, drawing people toward a shared vision. Your work becomes not just impactful, but transformational, leaving an unforgettable mark on those you serve.

Ambition is also a mindset—a way of seeing the world and your place in it. It is the belief that every day offers a chance to move closer to the impact you're meant to create. But this mindset can't survive on short-lived motivation alone. Ambition thrives on discipline—the consistency of showing up, doing the work, and staying focused on what matters most. Discipline turns small, intentional steps into monumental progress. It's the quiet power of persistence that allows you to navigate obstacles, stay true to your vision, and build the momentum needed to achieve ambitious goals.

At its best, ambition is a force that breaks barriers. It pushes you to think differently, take bold risks, and reimagine what's possible. Breaking barriers requires courage. The courage to act when the path is unclear, to persist when the journey feels overwhelming, and to lead with conviction even when others doubt your vision. Every barrier you overcome builds strength, resilience, and belief not just in yourself, but in those who are watching and learning from your example.

Ambition also empowers personal growth. It challenges you to take ownership of your journey and embrace opportunities that align with your values and vision. Whether you are pursuing advanced opportunities, elevating your influence in your current role, or leading from your current context, ambition calls you to make deliberate, strategic moves toward your goals. Personal growth fueled by ambition is intentional. It requires reflection, courage, and a commitment to continuous improvement. But more than that, it represents how your growth amplifies your ability to serve others. When you grow, you expand your capacity to impact, to inspire, and to create change.

Ultimately, ambition is about legacy. The most powerful ambition builds something that lasts. It creates opportunities for others, inspires new possibilities, and ensures that the work you've done continues to impact things moving forward. Legacy is shaped by the lives you touch and the contributions you make to a better future. Every step you take with ambition builds that legacy, creating a foundation for others to dream bigger, reach farther, and achieve more. Ambition is an invitation to see your work and your purpose through a lens of possibility and impact. As you reflect on what ambition means to you, consider the moments that have shaped your journey. What sparked your ambition? Who inspired you to move with purpose? Let's begin by exploring one of my own stories—an experience that clarified my understanding of ambition and how to make my dreams come true.

In 2017, I found myself sitting in the Superintendent's office at Middletown City Schools. It was my first day in the role. On the whiteboard in front of me was a single question:

"What ambitious move do you want to make?"

I posed this question not as rhetorical, but instead as an exercise in reflection. It was a challenge. A call to action. An invitation to step fully into the responsibility of leadership and make a move that mattered. I took that moment seriously.

A few weeks later, in late July, I brought our Executive Team together. I walked into the room with three portable whiteboards and dry erase markers. My first words were simple, but deliberate: *"We need to give people something they can believe in and something they can stand for."*

That day, we created what would become the heartbeat of our district: **#MiddieRising**. Together, we named the work ahead "*The Middie Modernization Movement.*"

At my first convocation, I introduced myself to the entire staff and community. Then I paused. I gave the staff two minutes to take out their phones, find their colleagues, and capture a #MiddieRising selfie. What may have seemed like a small moment was actually a strategic spark. It invited connection. It welcomed joy. It signaled that this district was stepping into a new chapter filled with purpose and possibility. From that day forward, #MiddieRising wasn't just a tagline. It was a mindset. A movement. A cultural identity.

We started seeing and hearing #MiddieRising everywhere throughout the district. The hashtag was on T-shirts, in social media posts, in hallway conversations. More importantly, we started feeling it. There was an energy that emerged. People were talking about the future again. There was pride. There was belief, and we had momentum on our side.

Of course, there was also resistance. Some told me changing the culture would be too hard. Others said we should just focus on improving test scores. I remember one staff member saying, *"We don't need a cheerleader. We need a leader."* That comment stuck with me. Because what they didn't yet realize was that leadership is about belief and inspiration. It's about making people feel connected to something bigger than themselves. I wasn't trying to hype people up. I was trying to build a foundation for change.

Over the next eighteen months, #MiddieRising reshaped the identity of our school district. I admit it was not perfect nor easy, but the ambitious move was intentional. And it worked. We gave people something they could believe in, something they could talk about, and most importantly, something they could contribute to. We moved with ambition, and the impact was undeniable.

What Moving with Ambition Looks Like

There are lessons within that story that go beyond branding or school spirit. They speak to what it truly means to *move with ambition*. Here's what moving with ambition really looks like:

1. **Acting with Bold Intentionality:** Ambitious people don't wait for the perfect moment. They create it. You don't need all the answers to make a move, but you do need intention. When we launched #MiddieRising, it wasn't about having a perfectly packaged plan. It was about sending a clear message: we're going somewhere, and everyone has a place in this journey.
2. **Igniting Belief in Others:** Ambition is about spreading energy. When people see that you believe deeply in something and them, it gives them permission to believe, too. #MiddieRising wasn't mine, but it became ours. The power of shared ambition is that it multiplies.
3. **Taking Strategic Risks to Shift Culture:** No culture ever shifted by staying comfortable. Change requires courage. Launching a movement means pushing against skepticism, against old narratives, and against the status quo. But when you take smart, intentional risks, you build credibility through action.
4. **Letting Your Values Lead the Way:** When critics questioned the movement, I stayed grounded in what I believed: our students and staff deserved joy, connection, and purpose. You move with ambition by standing in your values and inviting others to do the same.
5. **Turning Big Ideas into Visible Action:** Ideas are only as powerful as the experiences they create. From a whiteboard

question to convocation selfies to community conversations, we translated vision into visible action that connected to people. That's how you make momentum real.

My intent here is not to share a list of leadership tactics. They represent a mindset. A mindset rooted in the belief that bold, human-centered leadership can change systems, elevate culture, and unlock what's possible for others.

The Definition That Moves Us Forward

Here's what I want you to hold onto: To move with ambition is to find strength in the inspiration that lives in your heart, act decisively on what matters most, and stay deeply connected to your highest aspirations.

An ambitious mindset. It means we stop waiting for approval, and start moving with clarity. It means we listen to the fire inside us, the one fueled by purpose, not position. It means we create movements that outlive moments.

As you read this book, I invite you to reflect not just on what you want to achieve, but how you want to move. Your ambition is not too big. Your ideas are not too bold. Your purpose is not too much. The world needs more people willing to make bold moves, rooted in purpose, and fueled by belief.

> To move with ambition is to find strength in the inspiration that lives in your heart, act decisively on what matters most, and stay deeply connected to your highest aspirations.

The Four Key Principles: Purpose, Vision, Bold Agency, and Disciplined Consistency

When you see someone make a bold move, step into leadership with conviction, or spark a cultural shift in their company or community, it's easy to focus on the action. But behind every aspirational move is something deeper, an internal foundation made up of core beliefs that guide decisions, build resolve, and create consistency for the road ahead. When you truly connect with them, your ambition becomes grounded, durable, and transformational. We will ground the notion of *Moving with Ambition* in four key principles. Every ambitious move begins with a foundation strong enough to carry the weight of your goals, your growth, and your future impact. If you want to build a life, a career, or a legacy that reflects your highest aspirations, it is critical to root your movement in something deeper than just motivation. You need principles that serve as anchors to guide your decisions, stabilize your mindset, and sharpen your focus. The four principles at the heart of moving with ambition are *Purpose, Vision, Bold Agency,* and *Disciplined Consistency*. They are forces that are active, living drivers of your behavior that shape how you show up in the world. When aligned, they create a powerful internal framework for transformation and growth.

Purpose gives your ambition direction. It gives it meaning and connects your daily work to something bigger than a to-do list. Purpose anchors you in something bigger than yourself. It connects ambition to contribution. It makes your movement *meaningful*—not just impressive. Purpose is the fuel behind your ambition. It is the deeply held belief that what you're doing matters—and that your movement is in service of something larger than personal gain. Purpose affirms your choices and brings clarity to your voice.

CORE PRINCIPLES OF AMBITIOUS MOVEMENT

Vision is your mental map for where you're going. It's the picture of what's possible, the clarity of what success looks like, and the ability to imagine a future that excites you. It's what keeps you focused and serves as the mental blueprint of the future you're building. It's the clarity of where you're going and the ability to hold that picture steady, even when things get hard. Vision turns hope into strategy. It keeps you aligned to your highest aspirations. It gives your purpose direction, turning intention into motion.

Bold Agency is your willingness to take the lead in your own story. It's the decision to act with courage, even when the conditions might make you uncomfortable. Bold Agency means trusting your instincts, betting on yourself, and moving before you feel fully ready. People with bold agency are not looking for permission to make an impact—they create momentum through decisive action. Bold Agency is the belief that you have the power and responsibility to shape what happens next. It's the decision to move with clarity, conviction, and belief in your ability to lead change. It's courage in motion.

Disciplined Consistency is the daily practice that turns ambition into impact. Persistence is a survival mindset. What you need is a *movement* mindset anchored in discipline and steady execution. Disciplined consistency marries clarity, control, and compounding progress. It's the decision to do the small, essential things well over and over again. This principle is about the rhythm of your habits and mindset. Disciplined Consistency builds trust, creates traction, and ensures your ambitious moves are sustainable. Disciplined Consistency is the ability to stay committed to what matters most even when distractions, setbacks, or emotions threaten your momentum.

Think about someone you've seen make an ambitious move in your life. Maybe a friend who announced taking on a new job, a colleague who decided to start their own business, a leader who turned a company around overnight, or a teammate who stepped into a new version of themselves. If you look closely, you'll find those four principles at work. It was how they moved, what they believed, and how they responded to challenges. That same capacity exists in you. So the question now becomes:

What's the ambitious move you want to make?

Maybe it's advancing your career. Maybe it's shifting the way you lead your team. Maybe it's building something new, changing your environment, or simply showing up with more clarity and presence. Whatever it is, this is your time to define it and align it to the principles that will give it life. Ambition grows when we make it tangible, when we put language around it, and when we name the principles that will carry it forward.

So before you turn the page, pause. Not to reflect, but to explore and declare your next ambitious move. Here's an exercise to guide your thinking. Don't overthink it. Let your responses be real, unfiltered, and connected to your internal truth. This is about shaping the move you're going to make and grounding it in purpose, vision, bold agency, and disciplined consistency.

Ambitious Move Activation Exercise

1. **What is one bold, meaningful move you feel called to make right now in your career or life?** Describe it clearly. What makes it feel ambitious? Why does it matter?
2. **How does this move connect to your sense of *Purpose*?** Who will benefit from it? What values or convictions are fueling your desire to act?

3. **What does success *look like* for you in this move?** *(Vision)* What will be different when you've made progress? How will you know you're moving in the right direction?
4. **Where will Bold Agency be required?** What risks or decisions have you been hesitating to make? What bold step would move this forward right now?
5. **What does Disciplined Consistency look like for this move?** What daily or weekly actions could you commit to that will build momentum? What routines, habits, or systems will support you in staying focused?

Take your responses and sit with them. Revisit them. Read them out loud. This is your ambition, translated into structure. This process may feel small now, but don't underestimate what clarity can create. Clarity is the root of confidence. And confidence paired with intention is how ambitious moves take shape. Lead with it. Move with it. Let these principles shape the path forward.

Any career field or team setting offers the ideal space for people to move and influence their surroundings in their own authentic ways. Some of the best advice I ever received emphasized the importance of being yourself and doing the job in a way that celebrates what you offer others. The ambitious individuals who sustain success over time have something in common: they operate with a set of habits that serve as the foundation for their movement. These habits are deliberate and lived.

A teacher I know greets every student at the door with a handshake. That small gesture signals connection. A friend of mine, a school principal, always blocks out time at the start of each summer to reflect on her focus for the upcoming year. That simple practice represents clarity. As for me, I do everything I can to return every phone call, text, or email from someone who reaches out for support. I made a promise to myself: I will be an Encourager. Every day. In this profession, we have a surplus of critics. What we need more of are people who lift others up.

What I've learned over time is that these habits—these small, consistent actions—are the through-line in the story of ambitious individuals. They build credibility. They create energy. And they drive movement. One of my favorite thoughts to elevate my focus on the importance of consistency is something I wrote down before I ever became a superintendent: Allow your ambition to fuel your thoughts, and let your ambitious thoughts inspire new ambitious movements. That line reminds me that it all begins with discipline, the kind of daily discipline that aligns with your vision.

> **Allow your ambition to fuel your thoughts, and let your ambitious thoughts inspire new ambitious movements.**

Years ago, when I was a middle and high school principal at Mt. Healthy City Schools, a student named Ronnie told me I had one of the coolest last names in the world. He used to call me "Styles P" and would always say my leadership had a certain kind of swag to it. He meant it as a compliment, and he was right. Ronnie was a brilliant kid with so much potential, and I often found myself inspired by how he carried himself. After Ronnie graduated, I started keeping a list of habits that I believed would accelerate my growth and align my actions with my ambition. These weren't performance goals or productivity hacks connected to my evaluation. They were mindset shifts. Daily disciplines. Anchors. Over time, I refined and leaned into them, and they began to shape not just what I accomplished, but how I showed up in every space. I called them "Fresh Styles."

CORE PRINCIPLES OF AMBITIOUS MOVEMENT

Fresh Styles reflects what it means to bring your whole self into your ambitious journey; to live and lead with intention, connection, and the discipline to keep moving. A fresh approach to how you move and handle your business. These habits are a personal blueprint. A rhythm. A reminder that ambition doesn't thrive on talent or timing alone. It thrives on alignment. Fresh Styles is a collection of ten habits designed to help you align your daily actions with your purpose. They provide structure when the work is hard. They remind you that sustained momentum requires intentional effort. These ten habits map directly to the four core principles of ambitious movement that were introduced earlier in this chapter:

- **Purpose**
- **Vision**
- **Courage**
- **Persistence**

Each Fresh Style supports at least one of these principles, acting as a behavior-based anchor that helps bring them to life. They are how you live out your ambition in the quiet moments when nobody's watching. Let's walk through the four-phase arc of what these habits represent:

Phase 1: Rooted in Identity & Vision

This is where it starts. Before you can move with ambition, you need to know who you are and where you're going.

- **Stand for What I Believe** This habit reflects your core values and convictions. It keeps you grounded when others push back, and it defines your ambitious identity. Clarity in values builds credibility.

- **Dedicate Time to Think** Ambitious people pause, think, reflect, and strategize. This habit helps you regularly step back from the noise and think about who you want to become.
- **Strategic Patience** Growth doesn't happen all at once. Strategic Patience is the ability to trust the process, moving with milestones in mind, and knowing your opportunity will evolve itself over time. Putting the work in right now is what's most important right now.

Phase 2: Mastering Momentum & Discipline

Once you're rooted in identity, the question becomes: How do you move with consistency?

- **Celebrate Small Wins** This is where consistency lives. Celebrating progress and reaching milestones sustains motivation. It keeps the work joyful and visible, and reminds you that momentum builds one small win at a time.
- **Prioritize High-Impact Work** Not all work is equal. This habit forces you to focus on the projects and actions that truly move the needle on your readiness, your visibility, and your contribution.
- **Anticipate and Prepare for Moments** A successful journey is often defined by how you show up in critical moments. This habit builds foresight. It pushes you to look ahead, prepare thoughtfully, and deliver when it matters most.

Phase 3: Leading With and Through Others

You can't build anything meaningful alone. These habits focus on your relationships, influence, and service.

- **Build Relational Influence** Relationships are the bridge to trust. This habit challenges you to invest in others, encourage consistently, and show up with authenticity. It's how you create alignment and loyalty.
- **Do the Right Work to Serve People** Ambition becomes powerfully sustainable when it's grounded in service. This habit reminds you to align boldness with impact. Be sure you are doing the right work for the right reasons.

Phase 4: Sustaining Bold Ambition

Even the most successful ambitious people encounter resistance, burnout, and uncertainty. These habits help you push through.

- **Cultivate Resilience** You will face setbacks. This habit reminds you that toughness is a mindset, and that growth often comes from struggle. You can do hard things.
- **Adaptability in the Face of Change** Promises and commitments stay the same, but plans can and will shift. This habit builds the muscle to pivot with purpose and to see change not as a threat, but as a test of how bad you want it.

Over the years, I've watched incredible educators bring these Fresh Styles to life in ways that created powerful, lasting impact. While Superintendent at Middletown City School District in Ohio, I had a front row seat to watch how ambitious educators, community leaders, and administrators operated each day. A collection of observations has crafted my vision for a person or team that embraces Fresh Styles to move with ambition. I want to bring to the forefront some short stories that bring to life how Fresh Styles create spaces to function as an Igniter, Reformer, and Unifier. And their stories show what happens when daily behaviors align with purpose and bold vision.

1. **Fresh Style: Anticipate and Prepare for Moments**

    Mrs. Beadle and I were a wonderful two-person Communications team for several years. She was responsible for growing the one thing that represented our school culture, #MiddieRising. She grew the #MiddieRising brand, and did an amazing job. Mrs. Beadle approached me one day with a pretty bold idea. She opened the conversation by saying, "The moment we share this, it will bring people together." She wanted to team up with students to create a #MiddieRising movie that represented what #MiddieRising meant to them, and show it off to the community. She saw an opportunity to inspire the school community by offering them a moment to experience #MiddieRising. Mrs. Beadle put a plan together and executed it with precision alongside a number of others. We announced a Movie Premier Event titled *Middie XL*. She created a ten-second teaser video, and broadcast it across every communication platform imaginable to build anticipation. The #MiddieRising movie was professionally recorded and edited. When the final cut came in, Executive Team members were the first to see it. It brought tears to a few eyes. Middie XL arrived one January night at Middletown High School in the new arena. The entire community came out that night with an audience of almost 3,000 people. In the middle of the #MiddieRising movie, I paused to look around and to take in this moment that Mrs. Beadle anticipated. Mrs. Beadle is an *Igniter*. I often talk about offering people their moment of clarity and it will inspire commitment. Mrs. Beadle lived this Fresh Style to offer the community exactly that with the #MiddieRising movie.

2. **Fresh Style: Adaptability in the Face of Change**
   While visiting Creekview Elementary School during arrival on the first day of school, I got out of my car only to hear music playing. Now if you know anything about me, music fuels my soul. Walking through the parking lot, I had to walk around the front of a bus that was dropping students off. After waving to the bus driver, I turned my head to see this big speaker playing music outside the front entrance of the school. Students were skipping past, dancing, and giving high fives to the staff. With the goal of figuring out who was behind this great idea, I found myself connecting with Mr. Herald once again. He was a positive source of energy behind the culture of the building and did so much for the students, staff, and family. I absolutely loved visiting his classroom while at the school. That big energy showed up every single day for his students. I watched this amazing professional approach every single circumstance with curiosity while showing up with positive intentions. Through conversations with him, I discovered that no matter the district or building initiatives, or the focus from the Building Leadership Team, or a colleague wanting to start something new in the school, Mr. Herald remained adaptable in every case. The moment could require a shift in dismissal procedures or receiving feedback indicating opportunities for his students to demonstrate better success in math. He adapted every single time. Mr. Herald is a *Unifier*. His adaptability sparked positive interest from colleagues that ultimately shaped the culture of the building. I am sure students are still dancing their way into the school building while listening to his music.
3. **Fresh Style: Do the Right Work to Serve People**
   A friend of mine is always referring to me as a "Day One." I think that means I'm one of the original friends. Well, Mrs.

Morrison is definitely one of my favorite Day One friends and colleagues. Mrs. Morrison knew who she was as a leader and showed up every day as her cool and authentic self. I watched her commit to a belief and shape her behaviors to align with her belief system. She would always say it is important to "serve others and do it with truth and love." I have watched her mentor high school girls, cook pancakes for school celebrations, serve as a substitute teacher, serve on the board for a community organization, and experienced her challenge the work of the Executive Cabinet under the scope of: Does it serve the people? When she went to share her position on a critical move that was being considered, I had 100% confidence she came from a place of service to others. In her decision making, school design work, collaborations, and support, Mrs. Morrison lived in service to others. Mrs. Morrison is an *Igniter*, *Reformer*, and *Unifier*. She retired while we were on the same team in Middletown CSD. Although we avoided each other on her last day, she made it a point to remind me why we became educators. When we said goodbye, after working alongside each other for fifteen years, she came to my office door and said, "Remember you are here to serve others."

4. **Fresh Style: Celebrate Small Wins**

   Whenever I visited Mayfield Elementary, I was absolutely amazed as soon as I walked into the main office. Every single time, I was genuinely and joyfully welcomed by anybody who was in the office. On the counter, there would always be some type of staff game going on. I remember this wheel that you could spin and win a prize. The school constantly had celebrations for students, and the staff had this special energy about them. Reflecting back, I can put my finger on the one person who most inspired the culture of that building. Mrs. Keal, the principal, would be the person to celebrate here. As soon as I crossed paths with Mrs. Keal in the office or hallway, she would proudly share with me what was going on that day and what was planned for students and staff. My favorite was the staff potluck lunch that could always be found in the conference room. I would always sneak a few cookies. It brought me joy to see her celebrate the building, the students, and the staff. They held a students vs staff dodgeball game, had a dunk tank during field day, and decorate-the-door contests. In my six years of working with her, she never celebrated herself. Mrs. Keal was relentless in cultivating the sense of pride across the entire school. She valued every person, and took pride in how she invested in relationships with the staff. Mrs. Keal is an *Igniter* and a *Unifier*.

5. **Fresh Style: Strategic Patience**

    This story starts out in my first year as a superintendent with an ambitious elementary principal named Mr. Edwards. I found myself sitting across from him early in the morning eating breakfast and talking about his professional aspirations. Mr. Edwards had great command of his capabilities as an educational leader and the areas he wanted to further develop. Mr. Edwards' habits clearly represented a commitment to maximize his preparedness through strategic experiences, and he understood that over time he would be able to elevate his preparedness for any future opportunity. He expanded his network, gained new insights through the network, contributed to the negotiations team, attended a League of Innovative Schools convening, and shaped his approach to leading a department at the central office level. I observed him patiently preparing himself for over three years all while leading an elementary school. In my last year as Superintendent, Mr. Edwards served as the Senior Director of Human Resources. One would believe that he would be content with this new role, but not Mr. Edwards. His habits remained consistent as he advocated for new opportunities to develop as an executive leader. Mr. Edwards is a *Reformer*. He models how a commitment to evolving over time provides a major return on being able to celebrate what you have accomplished, where you are, and where you plan to go next.

What's most powerful about each of these stories isn't the title, the outcome, or the spotlight—it's the consistency of the habit. Each person lived a Fresh Style. And through that behavior, they elevated others, shaped culture, and moved with ambition.

Now it's your turn. Pause here, not to think about what you should be doing, but to reflect on who you are becoming:

- What kind of person are you today?
- What kind of person are you becoming?
- Which Fresh Styles already show up in how you live, work, and move—and which ones could unlock your next chapter?

This is where ambition gets personal. Not in what you hope for, but in what you do repeatedly when no one is watching. You don't rise to the level of your ambition, you rise on the strength of your habits. Ambition without action is noise. But ambition practiced daily becomes movement.

The person you're becoming is shaped by what you repeat, not what you imagine. So check in with yourself not just on your goals, but on your habits. Are your current behaviors aligned with the life, work, and impact you want to create? Do your daily moves reflect your highest aspirations? Your Fresh Styles are more than habits.

They are your foundation for meaningful progress, action, clarity, and growth. They're how you show up and how you start becoming the person your ambition has been waiting for.

You already have what it takes. Now the invitation is to align how you move intentionally–daily and unapologetically–with what you believe. The way you move creates the future you step into.

Position Yourself for Success: Taking Intentional Steps Toward Ambitious Growth

Breaking news: Success won't accidentally happen simply because you worked hard—it happens because you position yourself with intention. The ambitious educators in the previous section developed habits that kept them focused, but they also moved strategically, choosing their moments, environments, and relationships with care. This next level of growth requires more than discipline. It takes strategy. How might we place our work in the right rooms, alongside the right people, with the right timing? You could be doing incredible things behind the scenes, but if no one sees it, supports it, or connects it to something bigger, the momentum stalls. Positioning is how you make sure your effort turns into elevation.

When you learn to position yourself to be successful, you create your own opportunities instead of waiting for them. You start saying "yes" with intention and "no" with clarity. You recognize where you are, who you're with, and how you show up. Let's break it down and explore the strategies that can help you position yourself to be successful and move with ambition.

Understand What Sets You Apart

When you know who you are, you stop trying to compete and start choosing where you contribute. The most successful people aren't always the ones with the most credentials; they're the ones who are clear about what they bring to the table. Positioning yourself to be successful starts with recognizing your unique value. Here are three questions to help you uncover your edge:

- What have you consistently done well even when no one was watching?
- What do people thank you for or seek your advice on?
- What experiences have shaped your perspective in ways others may not share?

You don't need to be everything to everyone. You just need to be the best version of *you*. Whether it's your ability to stay calm under pressure, build relationships quickly, or turn chaos into clarity. Those are strengths worth owning. And once you own them, you can start making decisions that align with your identity. The more clarity you have about what sets you apart, the more confident and strategic you'll be in how you show up and where you choose to go next.

Be Selective About Opportunities

Not all work is created equal. Not every opportunity to prepare yourself through experiences is meant for you, and that's OK. The key is to approach opportunities with curiosity and intention. Ask yourself: *Does this opportunity help me grow in ways that align with my goals? Will it build the skills and experiences I'll need to move forward with purpose?* People who consistently position themselves for success are the ones carefully choosing what's worth their time and energy.

Let's be clear: success isn't measured by how many opportunities you take on. It's measured by how aligned those opportunities are with where you're going and who you want to become. It's easy to fall into the trap of saying "yes" too much and ending up stretched too thin. When that happens, distractions creep in, and they steal more than just your time, they steal your momentum. You start feeling like your calendar is full, but your progress is stalled. You may even find yourself thinking, *"I'm putting in all this effort…but where's the payoff?"*

That's when it's time to pause. To reflect. To ask yourself: *Is this work still connected to my purpose or am I chasing distractions instead of meaningful experiences?*

I've been there. I've had seasons when I believed that saying "yes" to every invitation and every project would accelerate my growth. But instead of growth, I found frustration. My days were busy, but not fulfilling. I wasn't moving toward anything that felt meaningful. It was only through reflection that I discovered a powerful truth: *Saying "no" is just as valuable as saying "yes."* Sometimes, it's the boldest and most strategic move you can make. Because when you say "no" to what doesn't serve your ambition, you create mental, emotional, and physical space for the opportunities that do. Trust yourself. When your vision is clear, and your habits are aligned, the right opportunities will find their way to you. And when they do, you'll have the clarity and capacity to say yes without hesitation because you'll know they're aligned with the future you're working toward.

Develop Depth, Not Just Breadth

In today's fast-paced world, there's a temptation to gather as many experiences and skills as possible in the hope it will equate to progress. But in reality, those who experience joyful ambition in their journey do so by acquiring depth through meaningful experiences. They choose to focus, go deep, and master specific areas of expertise that allow them to consistently deliver exceptional results.

Depth in ability is where you build your foundation of long-term success. Understanding it is not about skimming the surface of many subjects, but diving deep enough into one or two to truly understand, innovate, and lead. When you develop depth, you're acquiring knowledge and creating a skill set rooted in mastery. It requires intentional practice, reflection, and refinement. A key step to developing depth in your ability is identifying what you are passionate about and where you can deliver high impact. Ask yourself:

- *What topic excites me enough to want to understand it better than most people do?*
- *Where do I consistently bring value or offer something others rely on?*
- *Where do I see opportunities to solve problems and create solutions that others have overlooked?*

Sometimes ambitious people fall into the trap of thinking they need to do it all. But true success is often rooted in depth. Positioning yourself to be successful means going deep in areas where you can provide exceptional value rather than spreading yourself thin across too many initiatives. As you go deeper, you'll find value in the importance of doing the right work with greater precision. For example, instead of being involved in five different projects where you contribute marginally, imagine dedicating your time to a couple of high-impact projects where you can take ownership, explore challenges, and apply advanced problem-solving. This approach not only builds your expertise, but also amplifies your confidence because you understand the details, nuances, and intricacies that others may overlook.

Depth in your ability also leads to innovation. When you spend significant time immersed in a subject, you begin to see connections that others don't. You recognize gaps, patterns, and opportunities for improvement. That's when you transition from simply being skilled to becoming a problem-solver and reform agent. This perspective allows you to think beyond the basics, generate new ideas, and execute them effectively.

The more you refine your craft, the more opportunities you create for yourself. Let your knowledge and expertise run deep, and you'll discover that your newly developed capacity is more than an advantage—it's a differentiator.

Strengthen Your Personal Brand

A great reputation can open doors before you even knock. Positioning yourself for success requires much more than just doing good work—it means making sure that work is seen, known, and trusted. In today's world, visibility matters. You want people to know what you do, *how* you do it, and *why* it matters. Your personal brand is the signal you send to others. It's built through consistency in your actions, clarity in your values, and credibility in your results. When your habits align with your purpose, and your work consistently reflects your values, people begin to associate your name with impact. That's the power of a strong personal brand, one that speaks on your behalf, even when you're not in the room. But a personal brand is built with receipts. Successful people ensure their work speaks for itself. They deliver results. They build trust. They establish a track record of excellence that becomes their reputation. When the right opportunity shows up, people don't need to be convinced that you can do what it takes. They already know what you're capable of. Ask yourself:

- *What do I want to be known for?*
- *Do the things I do every day reflect that?*
- *What can I start doing (or stop doing) to make my values and strengths more visible to others?*

The most powerful personal brands don't need a perfect message. All you need is a consistent presence. When you show up with clarity and let your work speak through your habits, you build a reputation that invites opportunity, fosters trust, and sets you apart.

Foster a Proactive Mindset

Opportunities rarely wait for the perfect moment, and they almost never arrive with a warning. That's why those who move with ambition prepare themselves *before* they're asked. They build capacity now, so when the door opens, they're already equipped to step through it with confidence. A proactive mindset is grounded in two things: curiosity and discipline. Ambitious people ask themselves, *What's next?* What skills will elevate my impact? Where can I grow? They don't wait for a role or title to require more of them, they invest in their growth because they know the investment compounds over time.

> A proactive mindset is grounded in two things: curiosity and discipline.

This mindset is strategic. The most successful people intentionally build new capabilities before the need arises. They read. They reflect. They seek mentors. They test ideas. They lean into learning opportunities that stretch their thinking, because they understand that readiness is the result of deliberate effort. Being proactive also means taking ownership of your path. That might look like:

- Volunteering for a high-visibility project
- Initiating a conversation with a mentor about your next step
- Asking for feedback so you can better align your work with your aspirations
- Offering a solution to a challenge others are avoiding

Proactivity centers on doing the *right* things with foresight and intention. Possessing the ability to see around corners, anticipate what's coming, and making sure you're growing in the right direction. So ask yourself:

- *What's a skill I need to strengthen before my next opportunity?*
- *Where am I being passive when I could be taking the lead?*
- *What would it look like to take one bold step this week toward something I want, rather than waiting for permission?*

Create a Network of Encouragers

Think about how you build relationships before you need them. Success is rarely achieved in isolation. Behind every ambitious move is a group of people who believe in you, offer support, and create pathways for new opportunities. Those who consistently move forward in their careers and aspirations understand the value of a strong network built on trust, shared purpose, and mutual encouragement.

The biggest mistake people make is waiting until they need something to start building relationships. Consider how you build and nurture your network early, staying connected through meaningful conversations, acts of support, and a genuine investment in others. A network of encouragers is made up of people who celebrate your growth, challenge your thinking, and advocate for you in moments that matter. These relationships are cultivated over time through consistency, care, and presence. Encouragers do more than lift you up when you're down, they remind you of your purpose, your impact, and your next move.

One of the most valuable ways to strengthen these connections is to lead with generosity. Ask yourself: *How can I help others grow?*

Who can I support without needing anything in return? When you give freely, you create a dynamic of trust that becomes the foundation for long-term collaboration and opportunity. Mentors, peers, and sponsors each play a unique role:

- **Mentors** share perspective and experience. They ask hard questions, expand your thinking, and help you avoid blind spots. A strong mentor relationship is built on honest feedback, reflection, and mutual respect.
- **Peers** offer momentum. They walk with you, celebrate your wins, and hold you accountable when you start to drift. Your peers are your sounding board and sometimes your lifeline.
- **Sponsors** create visibility. These are the people who use their influence to open doors on your behalf. They believe in your potential and advocate for it in rooms you haven't entered yet.

Your responsibility within this network is just as important as the support you receive. Be an Encourager for others. Show up when it matters. Offer your insights, celebrate their progress, and be the person who helps someone else move with ambition. The more you invest in others, the more aligned and energized your own path becomes. Ask yourself:

- *Who are the encouragers in your life and how are you nurturing those relationships?*
- *Who are you encouraging, mentoring, or sponsoring in return?*
- *How intentional are you in showing up for the people who matter most to your growth?*

The relationships you build today will shape the opportunities that come tomorrow. Keep investing in the people who help you become the person your ambition is calling you to be.

Anticipate What's Next

How are you preparing today for tomorrow's opportunity? People who move with ambition are always scanning the horizon. They pay attention to signals of change and emerging trends. They ask questions that keep them forward-thinking: *Where is my field headed? What will this role demand in the future? What can I do now to be ready later?*

This mindset turns preparation into a daily discipline. They stay informed, build new skills, and refine their approach. Whether through books, podcasts, real-world practice, or meaningful conversations, they are consistently investing in their own evolution. Anticipating requires the courage to evolve. Even when nothing demands it immediately, they are sharpening their abilities, expanding their awareness, and strengthening their confidence for the moment the opportunity arrives.

They see preparation as alignment. When ambition meets timing, they are already in motion. While others are figuring out how to respond, they've already positioned themselves to be successful. Ask yourself:

- *What do you sense is changing in your work, your field, or your community?*
- *What skills will make you more valuable in a future role?*
- *What are you doing right now that your future self will thank you for?*

Opportunity favors those who are ready. The work you put in today becomes the edge you carry tomorrow. Whether your next move is around the corner or years down the road, the decision to prepare now is a signal of your ambition.

Success is built, not granted. It grows out of intentional preparation, repeated discipline, and an unwavering commitment to becoming more than your current role, your current title, or your current circumstances. Positioning yourself for success is the act of owning the process of aligning your behaviors, habits, and mindset with the future you are working toward. No one illustrates this more powerfully than Mr. Edwards.

When I think about what it truly means to position yourself to be successful, I go back to the early mornings, sitting across from Mr. Edwards, with scrambled eggs and water in hand, and conversations that always focused on the future. He never once talked about chasing a role. He talked about becoming ready for one. His aspiration was rooted in clarity and guided by discipline. He had a vision of the kind of leader he was becoming, and he chose to move with precision—building relationships, seeking feedback, contributing in spaces where his voice added value, and developing new dimensions of leadership that would serve him and his team later.

He didn't rush the process. He respected it. He led an elementary school with excellence while quietly expanding his impact across the district. From participating in high-level negotiations to representing the district at national convenings, Mr. Edwards was showing up in ways that shaped culture and improved outcomes. And he did it all with the patience to grow into the opportunity, rather than try to force it. His habits aligned with his ambition, and that alignment gave him momentum. When you build depth, make intentional choices, and surround yourself with people who believe in your potential, you begin to reshape what's possible. You stop operating on chance and start operating on purpose. Mr. Edwards built depth by identifying where he could contribute meaningfully. He wasn't trying to do everything. He focused on doing a few things well, and in doing so, he elevated his confidence and credibility. He asked questions that revealed the complexity of district leadership. He reflected regularly. And perhaps most importantly, he sought feedback that stretched his thinking. When the role of Senior Director of Human Resources became available, he stepped into it, fully prepared to take on the responsibility.

This is what it means to position yourself to be successful. To see growth as a responsibility, to treat your habits as investments, and to lead in a way that's rooted in value, not visibility. People will often say they're ready for the next opportunity, but readiness isn't a feeling. It's a pattern of behavior that proves itself over time. Throughout this chapter, you've explored how strategic patience, clarity, depth, personal branding, adaptability, and strong relationships all contribute to building that readiness. These are ambitious habits that compound over time. They help you navigate complexity. They prepare you for the unseen challenges ahead. And they allow your growth to create space for others to rise with you.

As you reflect on your own journey, think about the future you envision. Then look at your current moves. Are they aligned? Are you developing the habits that shape how you show up in high-pressure moments? Are you cultivating the relationships that challenge your thinking and open new doors? Are you investing in the areas of your life that will carry positive influence in the years to come? These questions matter because ambition without strategy leads to frustration. And strategy without belief leads to hesitation. Which is why now, the journey shifts. Once you've laid the foundation and committed to moving intentionally, it's time to build belief in the person you're becoming. That belief will be informed by the effort you've put in. It's reinforced by the habits you've built, the clarity you've gained, and the people who see what you're capable of even when you can't quite see it yourself. So as you begin Chapter 2, carry this truth with you:

MAKE YOUR MOVE

The person you are becoming is shaped by how you move today. Shaped by the clarity you cultivate in connection to your ambition and the belief you choose to act on every single day.

Now, let's talk about that belief. Let's name it. Let's build it. Let's move with it.

CHAPTER 2

Permission to Believe

Coming Together with Your Belief

I have watched a friend of mine lead for years. Her work transformed lives, including adults striving to advance their careers, families working to build a better future, and students discovering their passions in ways they never imagined. She led with calm strength and offered sharp strategic insight in every space she entered. And for the longest time, I kept wondering what her next big move would be. What bold ambition might be sitting just beneath the surface, waiting for the right moment? The mistake I made was focusing on the potential move, not the mindset. When I finally called her, not to talk about her potential big move, but to ask what she believed about herself—everything changed. She immediately started sharing how she committed to believing in herself every step of the way. I was so inspired by how critical self-belief is to her personal journey. Her comments caused me to reflect on the importance of having a personal belief system. From that conversation, three truths emerged:

- **Belief is What Carries You**
- **Belief Helps You Lead with Authenticity**
- **Belief Keeps the Mission Bigger than the Moment**

In that moment, I saw what it really means to "Come Together" with your belief. In Chapter 1, you began naming the ambitious move you want to make. You defined the habits that shape how you show up. You saw what's possible when strategy and discipline collide with conviction. But here, in Chapter 2, you turn inward. You explore *what you believe is possible* about your goals, your identity, your capacity, and your future. This is the inner alignment work that gives your ambition the power to endure.

Belief comes to life when you create space for it, and that space begins with presence—yours and the people around you. In this chapter, you'll embark on a journey to build something that can't be seen—but will shape everything you do: your **Belief Blueprint**. This journey focuses on constructing a deep, durable belief system that you can stand on no matter the moment. As you navigate Chapter 2, take time to begin building a few foundational components of your Belief Blueprint. A **Belief Blueprint** is the intentional design of the core convictions that guide how we think, act, and grow. Every ambitious move stretches us into new territory. That's why we must go beyond naming what we believe and start understanding how those beliefs shape our motivation, strengthen our resilience, and align our actions with our highest aspirations. It becomes the inner framework we return to when decisions get complex, outcomes are uncertain, and progress demands more of us. Built over time, it becomes your inner architecture: a structure of confidence, clarity, and alignment that helps you stay rooted in who you are while growing toward who you are becoming. Your Belief Blueprint guides how you show up, what you pursue, and how you respond to challenges

You will move through **four phases** of belief, each one building upon the last. These phases mirror the emotional and mental progression of ambitious growth. It starts with curiosity and connection, then moves into challenge and clarity, then commitment, and finally, conviction.

1. **Coming Together:** This is where belief begins to take root. You're surrounded by ideas, questions, and the energy of possibility. In this phase, you'll reflect on what inspires you, what you value, and what you're ready to move toward. You'll start to name your strengths and reconnect with the spark that led you to this moment.
2. **Building Self-Awareness:** This is a phase of self-discovery and affirmation. Doubt, discomfort, and resistance show up. You'll explore the power of owning your story, understanding your truth, and letting that truth shape how you see yourself. This is where self-awareness becomes your anchor, and where the real opportunity to connect with yourself begins.
3. **Committing to What You Believe:** Belief becomes movement when it is structured. Here, you'll transform your insights into meaningful commitment statements that clarify who you are, what you stand for, and what you're willing to pursue. This phase is about turning belief into a strategy you can act on.
4. **Strengthening Your Belief Daily:** Your belief strengthens when it becomes an "all the time" practice, and something you return to in the routines that define your days. You will explore how to protect what you believe in, and how to take pride in standing for what you believe and believing in what you stand for.

Blueprint Box Activities

The **Blueprint Box** is your invitation to pause, look inward, and gather the early building blocks of your belief system. These questions are guideposts meant to help you reconnect with the truth of who you are and what you're capable of becoming.

These activities are designed to help you reflect with depth and honesty. Each question opens a window into your past, your present, and your growing self-awareness. The goal is to surface the moments, people, and internal shifts that have already begun to shape your belief—sometimes without even realizing it. As you engage with the Blueprint Box, take your time. Rushing won't serve you here. Instead, treat this as a conversation with yourself—one that holds the potential to reframe your doubts, reignite your confidence, and remind you why your ambition matters. Write your responses, think them through quietly, or speak them aloud. However you choose to engage, let this reflection mark the beginning of your belief journey.

The Blueprint Box activity in this section is designed to help you build three core parts of your Belief Blueprint: **Identity Awareness**, **Affirming Influences**, and **Current Confidence Anchors**. These three elements form the foundation of belief that will support your growth throughout the rest of the chapter. Take your time to live with the questions because they can influence your awareness. Your reflections can help mark the beginning of your evolution from hopeful ambition to grounded, enduring movement. Building and/or affirming your belief system can accelerate the trajectory you are on to make that ambitious move. Let's begin where belief always begins: quietly, honestly, beneath the surface.

Coming Together is the starting point of your belief journey—a season of curiosity, connection, and self-discovery. In this phase, belief is not yet fully formed, but something within you knows it's time to begin. You're gathering experiences, values, memories, and truths that have shaped how you see yourself and what you hope to create. You're not alone here. This is where your identity, purpose, and potential begin to align—not in isolation, but through reflection, relationships, and reawakening the reasons why you care so deeply about the work you do. This first phase of the Belief Blueprint asks you to name what you're carrying with you right now and what you're willing to release. This is where you begin deciding to connect and choosing to show up with the mindset, energy, and curiosity that allow belief to take root. You're building belief in *why you're here in the first place*

This phase invites you to slow down and take inventory—not just of what you do, but who you are. What has influenced you? What gives you energy? What do you believe is possible for your life, your career, your team, and the lives you impact? When you bring those pieces together, you begin to see the outline of something powerful forming: a belief system rooted in authenticity. Allow yourself to reconnect with what matters most and give yourself permission to believe again—on purpose, with purpose.

A great deal of belief already lives within you. It just hasn't been activated yet. We've been conditioned to think belief requires bold speeches, perfect timing, or external confirmation. But belief is often invisible. It's built in subtle, repeated choices. So pause here. Before you move forward, look inward. Ask yourself:

- *What energy am I bringing into this season?*
- *What beliefs have I carried with me, even when things got hard?*
- *Who helped me believe before I believed in myself?*
- *Where am I still hesitant to trust myself and why?*

You may not call these moments "belief," but they are. And they matter. Start by noticing: What ideas are you still holding onto, even quietly? What challenges have you overcome that proved your resilience? What compliments or affirmations do others give you—ones you haven't fully accepted, but return to in your mind? These moments are evidence. And evidence, when acknowledged, becomes fuel for strengthened internal belief.

Blueprint Box: Coming Together As a starting point, use these prompts to reflect:

- Who or what helped you believe in your potential when you needed it most?
- What part of your self-belief feels strongest right now?
- Where are you hesitating to believe in your own potential?
- When was the last time you acted on something before you felt fully ready?
- What inner truth are you still learning to trust?

Here is the truth: Coming together with belief is deeply personal. No one can see it but you. No one can choose it but you. And yet, when you do, everything begins to shift. Belief is not the reward for success. It's the prerequisite.

> **Belief is not the reward for success. It's the prerequisite.**

Building Self-Awareness

The first stirrings of belief often come quietly—through a moment of courage, a surprising "yes," or a time you showed up before you felt ready. These moments rarely look extraordinary from the outside. But inside, they're transformational. They become the turning points and pieces of your story where you started finding your way toward who you truly are. This next phase is about recognizing and reclaiming those pieces. After curiosity and connection, the phase of building self-awareness invites you to explore the stories that shaped you. Not to dwell in the past, but to mine it for truth, for evidence, for strength. It's about discovering the lived experiences that built your confidence, stretched your capacity, and confirmed what you're capable of.

You've already made belief-driven decisions, even if you didn't name them as such at the time. Maybe it was the moment you asked for the opportunity you weren't sure you'd get. Or the time you kept going when everything in you wanted to quit. Or the time you led with honesty, even when it was hard. These are not just memories. They are proof.

Our stories shape our beliefs. We all carry personal narratives, and a lifetime of stories that we've told ourselves (or been told) about who we are and what we can become. These narratives have shaped our internal beliefs more than we realize. They have influenced how we show up, what we reach for, and how we respond when things don't go as planned. I would go on to say that some of our personal narratives have limited what we believed, while others have affirmed what we believed was possible.

But here's the truth: *You have the ability to choose the stories that shape your belief.* In this phase, you're invited to explore four powerful dimensions of your personal narrative:

- **My Worth**: What has taught me that I matter?
- **My Capability**: What has proven that I can rise, learn, and lead?
- **My Belonging**: When have I felt most seen, valued, and connected?
- **My Potential**: What do I now believe is possible for my future?

This exploration should push you to reclaim authorship of what has shaped your personal belief. Be sure to honor what is true about your lived experiences. Challenge yourself to decide what deserves to guide you forward. Your Belief Blueprint is only as strong as your self-awareness. This phase provides the foundation for your inner architecture. By reflecting on your lived experiences including the triumphs and turning points, the affirmations and the doubts, you're putting structure beneath your belief to ensure it stands firm and continues to evolve.

> *Self-awareness is what gives belief its shape, resilience, and staying power.*

Blueprint Box: Finding Your Way Through Story This Blueprint Box activity is your invitation to reflect on the moments, people, and choices that have influenced the belief you carry today. Let your answers be honest and unfiltered. Assume the mindset that you're writing to reconnect with what's real.

Prompts:

- *What part of your story has shaped your confidence the most?*
- *What choices have you made that surprised you with your own strength?*
- *What feedback or affirmation have you received that stuck with you—and why?*
- *What limiting narratives are you ready to release or rewrite?*
- *What moments proved your ability to adapt, lead, or persist?*
- *If you could rewrite the story you tell yourself about your worth, capability, belonging, or potential, what would it say?*

You are shaped by the way you've moved through your chapters in life and the meaning you choose to give them now. As you assume the role of storyteller moving forward, remember you are forging your way for the future on your own terms, with your own truth.

You have done meaningful work—quiet work that the outside world rarely sees but that shapes everything that follows. You have reflected on the belief that first stirred within you, revisited the stories that shaped your strength, and named the truths that are beginning to guide you forward. The first half of this journey has been about gathering, listening, and remembering. You now stand at a natural threshold in the process. Before you build the next layer of your Belief Blueprint, take a moment to honor what you have uncovered. Ask yourself what you are carrying forward with intention and what you are ready to leave behind. The space you create here, grounded in awareness and anchored in truth, becomes the foundation for the commitments you are ready to make.

Committing to What You Believe

The early phases of your belief journey asked you to turn inward, to listen carefully to the stories that shaped you, and to begin reclaiming what you know to be true about yourself. Those steps were about gathering. They were about honoring the strength already present within you and noticing how belief quietly formed across your lived experience.

Committing to What You Believe moves you into a new phase of this work. In this phase, belief begins to take visible shape. It shifts from reflection to intentional design. You are no longer simply noticing what is true; you are making decisions about how to carry that truth forward to drive you towards making your ambitious move. This is where you begin to design your Belief Blueprint by building a system strong enough to support the ambitious move you are preparing to make. In this phase, you will define three essential components: a *Core Belief Statement*, a *Fidelity Statement*, and a set of *Commitment Statements*. Each one plays a critical role in your Belief Blueprint. Together, they create a framework that links your internal conviction with your external ambition, ensuring that the bold moves you are preparing to make are fueled by something deeper than circumstance. The work you do here is the beginning of lived alignment and the process of translating who you are becoming into how you will move forward.

Building Your Personal Belief Structure

The framework you design in this phase is made up of three parts:

- **Core Belief Statement**
  This is the central truth you are choosing to believe about yourself, your mission, and your capacity to lead with impact. It shapes the identity you are building and becomes the foundation you move from as you pursue your ambitious move.

- **Fidelity Statement**
  This is the commitment to remain loyal to your belief when it is tested. It defines how you will protect and honor your core truth, especially when fear, distraction, or doubt try to pull you away.

- **Commitment Statements**
  These are the specific, consistent actions that allow you to live your belief daily. They are tangible steps aligned with your ambitious move—small but powerful practices that give internal conviction visible form.

Together, these elements create a living system: a belief-driven framework that can hold you through the complexity, uncertainty, and demands of real leadership and meaningful pursuit.

Example: A Belief Blueprint in Practice Earlier in this chapter, you reflected on the story of my friend, the leader who consistently carried her work with strength, clarity, and purpose, even before the world recognized the full scope of her impact. Her belief was shaped by intentional decisions to stay true to who she was, regardless of the noise around her. If we frame her journey through the structure of the Belief Blueprint, it would look something like this:

Core Belief Statement	Fidelity Statement	Commitment Statements
I believe I am capable of leading transformative change by staying anchored in courage, empathy, and disciplined action.	I will remain true to this belief by making decisions that reflect my values, even when uncertainty or success challenges my confidence.	Create space weekly for reflection and alignment.
		Initiate difficult conversations when clarity is needed.
		Prioritize building long-term value, not just immediate results.

Her belief was never just an idea she carried internally. It became a system she lived inside of daily, a structure that held her leadership steady across seasons of both ease and challenge. You are now invited to build the same kind of foundation—one that matches the weight of the ambition you carry.

Blueprint Box: Committing to What You Believe The work you are about to complete gives visible form to the belief you have been shaping within. These statements are the early architecture of how you will lead yourself through the ambitions, uncertainties, and opportunities ahead. Each statement you create becomes a decision to carry your belief forward with intention. The Core Belief Statement names the truth you choose to stand on. The Fidelity Statement anchors you to that truth when success or uncertainty challenge your confidence. The Commitment Statements translate belief into visible, consistent movement. Take your time as you move through each step. Build something real enough to return to when clarity fades, and strong enough to carry your ambition forward.

Step 1: Core Belief Statement

Prompt: What central truth are you choosing to believe about yourself, your mission, or your capacity as you pursue your ambitious move?

Begin with: *"I believe..."*

- **Example:**
  I believe I am capable of leading with clarity and purpose, even when the outcome is uncertain.

Step 2: Fidelity Statement

Prompt: How will you remain loyal to this belief when it is tested by uncertainty or success?
Begin with: *"I will remain true to this belief by..."*
- **Example:**
  I will remain true to this belief by aligning my decisions with my core values, even when external pressure tempts me to drift.

Step 3: Commitment Statements

Prompt: What consistent, tangible actions will allow you to live this belief daily and support the ambitious move you are building?

Begin each with: *"So I will..."*
- **Examples:**
  So I will block time each week to build the next stage of my vision.
  So I will seek feedback to sharpen my leadership and strategy.
  So I will encourage my own progress when setbacks happen.

Focus on actions you can practice consistently, not perfectly. Strength is built through steady movement.

What you have created here is the beginning of a belief system designed to move with you. These statements are not meant to sit on a page; they are meant to shape the way you move, decide, and grow. As you move forward, the work becomes more about practice than reflection. In the fourth developmental phase, you will strengthen the belief you have built by weaving it into your daily mindset, your decisions, and your way of pursuing the ambitions you have named. What you build now strengthens what you are capable of becoming later.

Strengthening Your Belief Daily

Have you ever stopped to think about the difference between things you practice professionally some of the time versus all the time? Belief deepens when practiced consistently. It is reinforced through steady alignment between what you say you believe and how you act. Every time you make a decision that reflects your Core Belief Statement, you strengthen your own credibility with yourself. Every time you honor your Fidelity Statement, you build resilience. Every time you follow through on a Commitment Statement, you confirm that your ambition is connected to something real. It is important to note that stacking small wins will absolutely elevate your confidence and belief. Choosing to stay connected to your belief in the daily work and actions is what transforms it to increased motivation and excitement about the possibility of being able to live your aspirations.

Carrying belief forward also demands attention during moments of momentum. Growth, achievement, and opportunity can sometimes cause drift just as easily as challenge can. When you begin to experience success, the temptation may arise to loosen your grip on the practices that grounded you. Belief must be protected not because it is fragile, but because it is essential. You built this system to last, and that durability comes from honoring it with consistency. Revisiting your Core Belief, checking your Fidelity, and living out your Commitments are ways to keep your ambition aligned with who you truly are, not just with what the moment demands. Belief carried with consistency shapes not only what you achieve, but how you become someone worthy of the ambition you hold.

> Belief must be protected not because it is fragile, but because it is essential.

Blueprint Box: Strengthening Your Belief Daily Your belief system gains strength through active reinforcement. Use this Blueprint Box to create a simple plan for how you will live your belief daily, guard it through seasons of momentum, and recommit when needed. Reflect and respond:

- **Belief Rally Cry:** Identify a short phrase, mantra, or rally cry that captures the belief you are standing on as you pursue your Ambitious Move.
    - *What words will you carry with you into the work ahead?*

- **Protection Plan for Your Belief:** Describe how you will protect your belief when challenges or success test your focus.
  - *How will you stay loyal to the belief that built this journey?*
- **All the Time Belief Practices:** List two or three things you will practice daily. These are all the time type practices that drive you toward that ambitious move.
  - *List and define the daily belief practices?*
- **Belief-to-Ambition Connection:** In one or two sentences, explain how your belief system prepares you to pursue your *Ambitious Move* with clarity and endurance.

Chapter 2 has been about building what lasts. This belief work began with a conversation that changed the way I saw growth and leadership. I am grateful to my friend for inspiring me to explore the importance of building a personal belief system—something deeper than confidence, something strong enough to move with me through every season of ambition. Together, we have learned that strengthening one's belief system is one the most ambitious moves you can make. As you move toward your ambitious goal, stay rooted in the belief that brought you here. You have already proven you can build something real. Now comes the moment to move with it, protect it, and trust it to take you farther than you imagined.

CHAPTER 3

Harness the Power of Discipline

Realities of Your Behavior

One of my favorite things about hearing the stories of other people is when they celebrate or brag about something positive that is happening. I wish more people and more teams would brag about the work they are doing. I like to say that if you appreciate your joy, then your joy will appreciate. When the grind feels good, be sure to take a moment to appreciate your journey. A lot went into tackling all those important milestones. In an attempt to remain motivated at all times, I like to take the mindset that "I am just off to a good start." This way I remember that sustained focus is essential to ensuring my effort produces the outcome I'm looking for. My advice to people and teams who are enjoying any degree of positive success is to "stay the course."

> If you appreciate your joy, then your joy will appreciate.

One of the most rewarding moments in the work we do is when someone takes a step back and genuinely acknowledges how far they've come. When a team speaks with pride about what they've built. When an individual reflects and recognizes that their commitment is starting to produce visible change. Would you agree that disciplined and intentional effort does, in fact, yield movement? Embrace that sense of pride with a unique pulse check. When the work starts to feel aligned with your purpose, pause long enough to appreciate it. Momentum becomes more sustainable when it's acknowledged with intention.

With that being said, there's a degree of confrontation that happens when you stop sugarcoating where you are and take inventory of how you got here. Sometimes it shows up on an ordinary Wednesday afternoon after a conversation in a meeting that didn't land, a moment when your production becomes inconsistent, or you receive feedback that indicates you still have room to further develop. I've had those moments more than once. The kind where you look around at your collective results, the missed opportunities, and you realize your effort hasn't matched your ambition.

Disciplined self-awareness is the skill that keeps you grounded in these moments. It's the ability to step back from the noise. Your **Current Reality** lives in the choices you've repeated, the priorities you've followed through on, and the level of seriousness you've brought to each day.

> ***Current Reality*** *is the outcome of your habits in motion, and how you are showing up for yourself. It represents the state of progress or disconnected movement that your recent decisions have produced. Whether you've been focused or distracted, steady or reactive, the reality around you is shaped by the follow-through behind your decisions.*

This is where a reality check matters not as a reflection, but to confront the difference between the effort required and the effort you've actually put forth. How often do you practice giving yourself a Reality Check? Take a moment to examine the last sixty days purely on your focus, behaviors, and consistency, *what position would you expect to be in right now? What would you expect, given the type of hard work you have or haven't put in?* Think about how you have honored the priorities you set. Do your actions reflect your stated ambitions or reveal the gaps between intention and execution? What patterns surface in your actions? How did adversity show up, and how did you handle it? The way you've invested your attention and energy becomes a tangible measure of your reality. Your Current Reality is a representation of what you've chosen, practiced, tolerated, or ignored. Take a look at the evidence and decide whether it matches the future you want. If it doesn't, the work immediately begins with different behavior, not a different goal. A different outcome always begins with a different level of follow-through.

This same tension shows up in teams. The ones that feel stuck are often ones that know they're capable of more. But instead of shifting the behavior, they try to shift the circumstances. They tell themselves things will improve when the pressure lightens or when more time becomes available. If the team's Current Reality matches this, it might be a good idea to reset the habits and terms. Choose a sixty-day window. No shortcuts. No excuses. Show up with the consistency your goal deserves. And when you reassess, you'll see the difference. *Your effort always tells the truth.*

Ideal Reality begins with imagination, but it becomes real when your actions start reflecting the seriousness of your aspirations.

> **Ideal Reality** *is what becomes possible when you lead yourself with discipline. It's a rhythm of movement where your habits reflect your values and your days move in the direction of your goals. This reality is a condition you build through intention, clarity, and the strength to keep choosing what matters most.*

This is a reality you build into existence—day by day, hour by hour, decision by decision. This version of reality forms through alignment, not from flawless execution, but from the steady commitment to show up with clarity and discipline. Alignment between your ambition and your habits. Your schedule and your priorities. Your words and your actions. When those align, Ideal Reality starts becoming a place you live. Have you experienced this rhythm? The feeling when your output matches your intention, and things begin to move with clarity? The meetings are sharper. The relationships are stronger. Thinking is more strategic. Not because everything is easier, but because you're no longer working against yourself. You begin to recognize yourself in the vision you've been chasing. The day has structure. The energy is steady. And the outcomes, while never guaranteed, begin to mirror the seriousness of your discipline.

But Ideal Reality is fragile when ambition is conditional. I've had seasons when I said I was committed, but if you had followed me around for a week, the evidence would've told a different story. While Executive Director of Curriculum and Instruction at Lakota Schools, I went through a period when I would visit classrooms, and got back in my car admitting to myself the only thing I accomplished was being visible. Ideally, I should have established look fors and key outcomes for the classroom visits to enhance my ability to make strategic decisions at the district level. That's what candid vulnerability looks like—admitting when your patterns don't reflect your potential.

For anyone—or any team—who is reaching for something more, the difference between Current and Ideal Reality is a signal. If there's distance between where you are and where you want to be, it's not a reason to retreat. It's a reason to realign. The most important thing is to adopt the mindset that your next move matters. Not just the visible one—but the internal one. The decision to re-enter the work with sharper focus. The choice to stop negotiating with your ambition. The commitment to a dedicated period of forward pressure that builds into a reality you can believe in. Approach this with the practice of candid vulnerability, where you provide yourself the unfiltered truth about how you are showing up. Enter this exercise with maturity,

> If there's distance between where you are and where you want to be, it's not a reason to retreat. It's a reason to realign.

a steady sense of purpose, and the belief that self-correction is part of growth.

Closing the gap between your Current and Ideal Reality requires more than insight; it demands disciplined action. The path forward involves creating clear, structured commitments. If you're serious about bridging this gap, commit with intentional effort. Align your daily behaviors directly to your stated priorities. Say "No" firmly to distractions that don't serve your vision. Show up with consistency and clarity each day. As a next step, you'll need signals that show you're actually gaining ground. What if the clarity you need next is hidden in the markers you choose to define your progress? And what if those markers are the first proof that you're having success in positioning yourself to be successful for what's next?

Momentum Markers

There comes a time during that ambitious journey that the excitement starts to fade and the weight of actually pulling it off just feels heavy. Do you remember when I shared that Mr. Farmer taught me the power of being prepared? As I have embarked upon a number of journeys over the years, I've learned that you must have a plan for how you are going to get to where you want to be. I have also learned that generating momentum early and often really impacts my mindset throughout the journey. Embracing both of these aspects inspires you to stay connected to the necessary work it takes to make progress toward your ambitious goals.

What is momentum? Momentum is created when effort to execute a plan begins to reflect the seriousness of your ambition. It takes shape through consistent follow-through, the kind that turns strategy into outcomes and intention into visible results. You begin to feel momentum when the actions you've committed to start generating exciting movement in the direction you planned. Each completed step builds credibility with yourself, reinforcing that your ambition is an idea in motion. Over time, that movement becomes self-sustaining. Progress compounds. Belief solidifies. And the effort you're making begins to create the conditions for what's next.

Momentum Markers bring attention to the outcomes that matter most on your journey. They serve as strategic proof points that signal progress and strengthen confidence. When chosen with purpose and sequenced intentionally, these outcomes serve as signals that your actions are generating momentum and having an impact on how you are positioning yourself to be successful. Let's strategically establish your Momentum Markers.

Mapping Your Momentum Markers: A Strategic Experience

Step 1: Reconnect With Your Ambitious Move: Start here. Before you set outcomes, return to the bigger move you're preparing for. What are you pursuing? Be clear. Your Momentum Markers are only valuable if they serve this future.

Prompt: Write a short statement that defines your *Ambitious Move*.

_____

_____

_____

Step 2: Identify Areas Where You are Already Positioned for Success: Confidence builds when you recognize the ground you've already covered. Look for areas where you've already built credibility, relationships, momentum, or preparation. These strengths are the starting points for your next moves. Attach an artifact to support each area.

Prompt: What areas or accomplishments give you traction right now?

1. _____

_____

    a. Artifact:

    _____

    _____

    b. Artifact:

    _____

    _____

2. _____
   _____

   a. Artifact:
   _____
   _____

   b. Artifact:
   _____
   _____

3. _____
   _____

   a. Artifact:
   _____
   _____

   b. Artifact:
   _____
   _____

Step 3: Identify Areas Where You Need to Better Position Yourself: Strategic progress often starts where you feel least ready. These are the areas that need more clarity, visibility, skill, or alignment. Be honest—not critical. This is where you can gain strategic ground and growth. Attach an artifact to support each area.

Prompt: Where do you need to strengthen your how you are positioned?

1. _____

   _____

   a. Artifact:

   _____

   _____

   b. Artifact:

   _____

   _____

2. _____

   _____

   a. Artifact:

   _____

   _____

   b. Artifact:

   _____

   _____

3. _____

    a. Artifact:

    b. Artifact:

Step 4: Define Your Momentum Markers: These are your signals of accomplishment and progress. Momentum Markers are outcomes—not tasks—that show you're strategically positioning yourself to succeed. They should be specific, connected to your ambition, and meaningful to your growth. There is no perfect number. Choose the ones that matter.

Prompt: List your Momentum Markers. Write as many as you need.

1. _____

2. _____

3. _____

Let me start by saying this: the fact that you're here, right now, thinking seriously about your ambition and your future? That matters. That speaks volumes. You've just gone through the process of designing something many people never take time to create—a plan rooted in purpose, built to move you forward, and designed to help you track your own momentum. That plan is a signal that you are ready to move forward with courage. You are creating the conditions for progress. You've named what matters, and you've outlined what it will take to move. That makes you dangerous to anything that tries to hold you back.

There's a phrase I believe in deeply: Your ambition doesn't need an audience. It needs your attention. Not every step will be seen by others. But every step will be felt by you. You will notice when you're doing the work.

> Your ambition doesn't need an audience. It needs your attention.

You'll recognize when you're slipping into distraction. You'll feel the difference between alignment and activity. That awareness will become one of your greatest assets.

Momentum Markers do something else that matters: they break the big into something you can act on. They make that ambitious move actionable. They give you a place to start. They let you see your own movement before anyone else does. You don't have to wait until all your Markers are complete to believe in your own progress. Let the first win be enough to keep going. Let the second win raise your standard. Let the third create momentum that doesn't just carry you forward, but begins to shape what comes next.

There will be moments when your original plan doesn't hold. When priorities shift. When obstacles appear. It just simply means you're in it. It means you're living the process instead of admiring it. Build in space to reflect, adjust, and reset. Your Momentum Marker map is a guide, not a contract. Use it to stay grounded in your purpose, but don't be afraid to rework the steps when something needs to shift.

Get to work on your first marker. Collect your evidence. Celebrate the win. Then repeat. That's how momentum is created. That's how belief is earned. That's how future opportunities begin to find you. And when they do, you won't be surprised. Because you worked for them. Don't wait for the opportunity to prove you're ready. Move like someone who already is. This plan belongs to you. So does the movement. So does the success.

And just so we're clear—this is the part that matters most. Not what you wrote down. Not what you hope to see happen. But what you do next. The next move belongs to you. As you work to build momentum behind your ambition, there comes a point when it's necessary to pause and evaluate the path you're on. Preparing yourself to be successful starts with a clear understanding of how your habits and actions are shaping the direction you're moving. The work you've done to define your habits and set strategic milestones now becomes the lens through which you assess your readiness to move forward.

> Preparing yourself to be successful starts with a clear understanding of how your habits and actions are shaping the direction you're moving.

This section introduces the High-Impact Preparation Index—a tool designed to help you evaluate how well your daily behavior and long-term execution are working together. It reflects how well you are preparing yourself to be successful. It captures how consistently you live your Fresh Styles and your ability to deliver on the milestones that matter. When both are present, your preparation creates a positive movement that you can celebrate. It becomes easier to stay focused, recognize progress, and respond with confidence to the challenges ahead. This index is a tool to help you measure how your current preparation efforts align with the future ambitious move you're working toward. There are two components:

1. **Work Rate**

    Work Rate is how often you choose to act in alignment with your ambition—on purpose, with discipline. It reflects how seriously you take the habits (Fresh Habits) that carry your goals forward. A strong Work Rate shows up in the details: how you start your day, how you push through resistance, how you protect your time, and how you finish what you start. This is where your daily choices show whether you're truly moving or just hoping.

Work Rate Self-Assessment Scale: *How consistently am I living my Fresh Styles (daily habits of ambition)?*

Work Rate Score (Scale 1-4)	Description
1	I rarely reflect on or practice my Fresh Styles. My habits often feel reactive or inconsistent.
2	I'm aware of my Fresh Styles, and I try to live them—but I struggle to sustain them across a full week.
3	I actively practice several Fresh Styles. I can point to routines and behaviors that reflect consistent discipline.
4	My Fresh Styles are deeply embedded in how I show up. They shape my days, decisions, and the energy I bring to the work.

2. **Progress Pulse Check:**

Progress Pulse Check reflects how effectively your efforts produce meaningful progress. It's measured by your ability to set clear milestones, take strategic action, and accomplish the milestones you set. A high contribution rate shows that you are moving in sync with your ambition—making tangible progress and fulfilling the outcomes you committed to.

Progress Pulse Check Self-Assessment Scale: *How consistently am I hitting the strategic momentum markers that define my progress?*

Progress Pulse Check Score (Scale 1-4)	Description
1	I haven't clearly defined my momentum markers, or I rarely take action toward them. Progress is hard to track.
2	I've set some momentum markers, but I struggle to follow through consistently. A few have moved forward.
3	I've achieved several of the strategic momentum markers I've set. My progress is visible and directional.
4	My momentum markers are clear, and I'm consistently delivering. Each one builds momentum aligned to my goals.

High-Impact Preparation Index (HIP)

The High-Impact Performance Index reflects how prepared you are to follow through on your ambition. It blends two core indicators: your Work Rate—the habits you live by each day—and your Progress Pulse Check—the progress you're making on the milestones you've committed to. Together, they indicate a disciplined approach, intentional progress, and momentum building toward what you want to accomplish. This index helps you see the full picture of your performance: Are you showing up the way you said you would? Are you advancing toward the future you're working to create? Use it as a checkpoint, a recalibration tool, and a signal of how prepared you are to deliver on the ambition that's guiding you.

High-Impact Preparation Index: Work Rate + Progress Pulse Check (out of 8): *How well am I positioning myself to be successful right now?*

High-Impact Preparation Index (Scale 1-8)	Description
1-3	You may be drifting. Take time to reflect, reset, and realign your habits and goals.
4-5	You're moving, but not consistently. Strengthen either your habits and/or your strategic execution.
6-7	You're operating with momentum. Build on it by refining focus and removing distractions.
8	You are fully aligned. Stay disciplined, track impact, and prepare for what's next.

The High-Impact Preparation Index is most valuable when it leads to movement toward your ambitious move. This index gives you the clarity to understand where you stand and the motivation to move with greater intention. It offers a clear picture of how your habits and execution are shaping your trajectory. High scores affirm that your daily behaviors and long-term execution are aligned. Lower scores reveal areas where renewed focus can create traction. Either way, the index prepares you to take deliberate steps forward. In the next section, you'll begin connecting that preparation to the concepts of making progress and building momentum.

There comes a point in every ambitious journey when progress matters more than plans. Where positive movement needs to be visible in your own lived experience. That moment consists of effort, strategy, reflection, and an honest relationship with how you're showing up. This is where strategic agency comes to life. Strategic agency is the practiced ability to claim ownership of your path and make decisions about what is best for you.

Strategic Agency enables you to assess where you are, anticipate what's next, and take meaningful action that positions you closer to your ambitions. Strategic agency is personal responsibility fused with forward-thinking execution. It means owning the full picture of your decisions, actions, results, habits, and mindset while interacting with the realities of your process in real time. You start noticing patterns in your effort. You see where your energy is paying off and where it's lacking. You get clearer about what's working and what isn't. And in that clarity, you unlock a new level of purpose driven movement.

> Strategic agency is the practiced ability to claim ownership of your path and make decisions about what is best for you.

To help track and strengthen that movement, we introduced the High Impact Preparation Index (HIP), a way to see how well your current behaviors align with your most important goals. Recall it holds two reflection scores: your Work Rate—*How consistently am I living my Fresh Styles? (daily habits of ambition)*, and your Progress Pulse Check—*How consistently am I hitting the strategic milestones that define my progress?* Let's lean into the practice of how to interact with your HIP Index score, and how it can be an influence on how you think about your next set of short-term moves. It is important to note that the frequency in which you look at the HIP Index score for feedback is up to you, it should be a source of inspiration.

Progress becomes most meaningful when it's personal. It's one thing to create a plan. It's another to interact with it in a way that builds belief over time. The HIP Index wasn't designed to be a quick self-check. It's meant to become part of your rhythm. Something you return to—not out of obligation, but because you're committed to making your ambition real.

There are ways to build that rhythm. Some leaders create a private routine that works with the pace that feels right for them. A friend of mine who is an accountant writes down the three behaviors that connect most directly to what he is trying to accomplish for the week. At the end of each day, he adds a quick note beside each one. "Moved on this." or "Slipped on this." or "Didn't even think about this today." There's no scoring system. Just awareness. That habit helps him stay grounded in what is important to him, especially when the work starts to pull him in competing directions.

Others anchor their HIP Index into more structured routines. A Human Resource Director turned her Thursday afternoons into a standing meeting with herself. For thirty minutes, she sits down with her calendar, her Momentum Markers, and her HIP Index from the week. She scores herself truthfully. And then she writes two questions in the margin: "What's this telling me?" and "What's one decision I can make now that helps me finish the week out right?" That small move has become a practice that helps her lead from strategy.

For someone else, the routine might be less formal. The goal is to find ways to stay aware of your effort, your results, and the patterns that are forming between the two. There's power in being able to see your own progress. Recognizing your own movement is one of the strongest motivators for strengthening belief and self-correction. That's also where strategic agency starts to feel real. You recognize when you're chasing tasks instead of outcomes. You begin to trust your ability to lead from a deeper place of alignment.

Strategic progress requires strategic awareness. At this point, I want to stress that I'm not pushing you to become a different person. The intent is to focus on how you are positioning yourself, and to determine if all the hard work you are doing is producing the desired progress you are looking for. The encouragement is to take ownership of how you intentionally, consistently, courageously, and honestly monitor your progress. Choose a cadence for reflection that fits your context—daily, weekly, biweekly. Monitor the gap between what you're doing and what's making a difference. Give yourself permission to adjust when you just are not executing the way you want. And when you see that score rising, pause to recognize the progress. Let that recognition be a source of energy, not a reason to ease up.

Design your own system to help you engage with different moments throughout your journey with the sole intent of not being perfect, but proactive. Commit to learning how to measure progress in a way that feels real. How can measuring progress become a habit for you moving forward? Want to move your ambition forward? Commit to doing the work. One measured step at a time.

CHAPTER 4

Navigating the Ambitious Journey

The Ambitious Move

Setbacks will test everything you believe about yourself. Sometimes your gut warns you that one is coming. Ever apply for a job and quietly start bracing for the rejection? Setbacks have the potential to steal your confidence, shake your identity, and leave you asking, "Am I built for this?" They can disrupt everything—even the parts of your journey that once felt so right. Adversity finds a way to introduce itself to us all and make us really think about what we do after the disappointment lands. I want to take you into a moment from my own story—a moment that forced me to confront my most ambitious professional desire to date. Before you move on, take a breath. Think about the last time a setback left you stunned, frustrated, or unsure. I share this story as an invitation: to see yourself in it, and to draw your own lessons for how you'll choose to respond the next time you face a setback.

In May 2017, I was hired as the Superintendent of Middletown City School District (MCSD). From the moment I stepped into the role, the heartbeat of #MiddieRising was real. We quickly began living our passion to evolve our school system so students could enjoy life changing successes. We were building belief in what was possible. The work, the people, the culture we were building together was the kind of experience every professional hopes to be part of at some point in their career. Our back-to-school convocations were off the charts. By the winter of 2021, I felt like we were thriving. Every decision I made was shaped by the pride and gratitude I felt for the students, staff, and community I served. I wasn't looking for a way out. I was living inside a purpose that meant everything to me. I loved being a superintendent. I loved being the superintendent who got to serve the staff, students, and community of Middletown City Schools.

That winter, the Cincinnati Public Schools (CPS) district announced it was seeking a new superintendent. It caught my attention, but not because I was dissatisfied or restless. The announcement stirred something deeper. I had been holding onto a commitment to serve and impact the education profession on a much greater scale. A sense that there were new communities, new students, new challenges waiting for a leader willing to answer a bigger call. I found myself sitting with hard questions: Was it time to move? Had I given #MiddieRising everything I had to give? Was my ambition dominating my thoughts or distracting me? Was I prepared to take on the new role? How did I feel about letting go of something I loved? Wrestling with these questions was very emotional. The thought of leaving MCSD surfaced deep emotions. I realized I had grown to love the staff and the students.

The process of deciding to apply wasn't made lightly or quickly. It came after days of reflection, conversations with those I trusted, and deep honesty with myself about my interest in making an ambitious move. I wrestled with it privately, carrying the weight of gratitude for what we had built and a rising sense of responsibility for what could still be built beyond it. My decision to apply was about honoring the original reason I chose leadership in the first place — to serve, to build, to impact lives. Applying for the superintendent role at CPS was a step into that possibility. It was the first bold move in a journey that would teach me more about resilience, belief, and comeback than I could have understood at the time.

The thought of applying for the CPS position stayed with me longer than I expected. It wasn't excitement that kept pulling at me; it was something quieter, something more persistent. It was the question that every leader who loves their work eventually faces: Have I given everything I have to the place that trusted me?

There were moments when I thought about staying and finishing what we started, staying until every goal was realized, every dream fulfilled. So many times other people would tell me they wanted to "see the work through" when they were considering other job opportunities. I found myself saying the same thing in my mind. For me, those thoughts came from a place of loyalty and gratitude, not fear. But leadership is not just about honoring where you are. It is also about honoring where you are being called to go. The weight of the decision never left me completely, even after I decided to apply. It was a moment of deep reflection — a step taken with full awareness that ambition carries a cost, and that courage sometimes means opening yourself to the possibility of goodbye.

Making the decision to apply was one of the most emotional choices of my career. It was made through slow reflection, through trusted conversations, through wrestling with the responsibility that comes with leadership. The weight of gratitude never left me. The love for the people of Middletown never faded. But my ambition was real, and the aspirations I had carried for years were real, too. I had spent years encouraging aspiring educators and leaders to pursue their boldest ambitions with courage. I took pride in pouring into them, and celebrating the opportunities they earned. It felt good to see others succeeding. This time, it was my turn to take my own advice–and trust the belief I had worked so hard to build.

Once my application was submitted, the process of moving forward began quietly. The early rounds of the CPS Superintendent search were intentionally private, designed to allow candidates to step into the process without public pressure. For me, that privacy was necessary. It gave me space to stay anchored in the belief that had brought me to this moment. I wasn't campaigning. I wasn't positioning. I was showing up fully as myself, trusting that the work I had committed my life to would speak louder than anything I could package or rehearse.

The early conversations, interviews, and written submissions demanded more than professional answers. I wanted to show the search firm and Board of Education who I was as a leader, but more importantly, who I was as a person committed to serving a community. My strategy was to convince them in every phase of the process that I was the right person to lead the people of CPS. After the screener, I debated if I should shift my strategy to showcasing myself as the right fit for the Board of Education. Ultimately, I decided to double down on my strategy that I was the right person to lead the people. Every question, every prompt became a test not just of experience, but of conviction. I reminded myself often that my greatest responsibility was to be the most authentic candidate. I remember sitting in a Zoom waiting room before an early virtual round, and reminding myself to carry purpose into a place where it could serve.

Privately, the emotional tension deepened. There were moments of genuine excitement, thinking about the scale of impact, the thousands of students, the educators and leaders who deserved to believe in what was possible for their future. There was real anticipation about the idea of bringing everything I had built and learned at Middletown into a new community ready for its next chapter. But alongside that excitement, there was also heartbreak. Every step forward into the CPS interview process meant a step further from the people I loved in Middletown. Even when no one else knew what was happening behind the scenes, I was already carrying the reality that if this door opened, it would come with both pride and loss.

I was honored to make it to the semifinalist round for the search for the Superintendent for a large school district. The finalist stage was quickly approaching, and that is where I learned how to handle setbacks. On January 27, 2022, the news became public. Cincinnati Public Schools announced the finalist list for the Superintendent position, and my name was included. In an instant, what had been a quiet, internal journey became visible to the world. The conversations I had been holding privately in my heart now had a public audience. The reality I had been preparing for privately–the possibility of leaving Middletown–was no longer something I could keep to myself. It was real, and it was now part of how others would see me.

The public announcement shifted everything. Inside the walls of Middletown City Schools, there were questions. There were conversations. There were people who felt pride, people who felt sadness, and people who wondered what the future would hold. I felt all of it with them. Walking into buildings where every handshake and every smile had once been about relationships now carried a different connection. I could feel the change in the air because the bond we had built was strong enough to feel the tremor of change before it even arrived.

The finalist process moved quickly, but every moment inside of it demanded focus, belief, and resilience. Being named a finalist meant stepping into a gauntlet of interviews and conversations that tested not just my preparation, but the foundation I stood on as a leader and person. Over two intense days, I would meet with groups representing every corner of the CPS community. Day one

I met with five different stakeholder groups. The last stakeholder group was streamed live to the public:

- Certified Staff
- Classified Staff
- Site Administrators
- Community Members
- Students

With precision, I stuck to my strategy of offering a leader who would be there to serve people. From the moment the first round began, it was clear that this wasn't just about answering questions. It was about embodying the values, aspirations, and leadership principles I had spent years building. I leaned heavily on my belief system–the personal architecture of conviction, courage, and service that had carried me through every challenge in my career. Each round of interviews required emotional resilience. Some groups were energized and hopeful. Some were skeptical and guarded. Some were looking for inspiration; others were looking for assurances. I completed the gauntlet and walked to the parking lot late that night with my head held high, very proud of what I offered the people of CPS. At the start of the day, I texted myself two questions to answer at the end of the gauntlet: *Were you authentic? Did you win the day?* When I got in my car, I answered both "Yes" to both questions.

On day two, I found myself walking into a room as the last candidate the Board of Education would interview. This meant that after I finished, it would be time for them to make their selection. Meeting with the Board of Education brought another layer of intensity. During the previous two and a half months of interviews, I paid exceptionally close attention to what the Board of Education was looking for. So in this final interview, I knew this was about one single question: Is Marlon Styles the right fit for CPS? There are two parts to the question:

1. Is Marlon Styles the right fit for the staff and students?
2. Is Marlon Styles the right fit for the Board of Education?

This was the culmination of everything. The chance to represent the heart behind the work and the hope behind the vision. As I walked into that final conversation, I carried with me everything Middletown had given me: the lessons, the gratitude, the spirit of service that had been built moment by moment, year by year. No matter what happened next, I knew I had stayed true to who I was. I had honored the people who believed in me by believing fully in the mission I carried forward.

When the final conversation concluded, I walked out knowing that I had left everything on the table. I had carried my belief system, my aspirations, and my commitment to service into every room. What came next was out of my hands. That evening, I waited for a call that never came. No updates. No decisions. Just silence. I knew enough about the interview process to understand that sometimes no news tells its own story.

The next morning, I visited Creekview Elementary for my regular school visits. The familiarity of connecting with the students and staff grounded me that morning. After the visit, I drove down Central Avenue, preparing to cross through the heart of Middletown like I had done countless times before. As I approached an intersection, the light turned red and my phone rang. It was a Board member from CPS. The Board had made its decision, and I had not been selected. I thanked the Board member for the opportunity. I wished the entire CPS community the very best as they moved forward.

The call was brief. It did not need more words than it held. Leadership, especially at moments like this, calls for gratitude over a reaction. As I hung up the phone, I sat for a moment at the light, feeling the weight of the decision settle in. There was no anger. Only a steady realization that the setback was part of the journey, not the end of it. Reflecting back, the best thing I did early in the process was prepare myself for either outcome. I made a promise to myself when I pulled into the MCSD Central Office parking lot. I promised to hold my head high, not allow my self-belief to waiver, and to continue serving others. I knew I had to do the emotional and mental work of facing this setback head on.

On February 28, 2022, an article was published titled "Middletown City Schools Superintendent Passed Over." In the days that followed the call, I stayed focused on the work in front of me. Every student I greeted, every conversation I had with staff, every decision I made reminded me why serving people mattered. I reflected on my decision to present a leader positioned to serve the people versus presenting a profile of a leader that was a fit for the Board of Education. I found peace in my heart and my mind that I interviewed as my authentic self as someone who sits in leadership positions to serve others. But beneath the surface, a deeper shift had started. I had given everything I had to the process. I had honored the mission and the people who had shaped me. And still, the opportunity did not open. Making an ambitious move demands that we face those moments honestly. Not with self-pity. Not with resentment. With the kind of clarity that only adversity can sharpen.

The setback did not shake my belief in what I was capable of. It did, however, push me to ask harder questions about what I truly wanted next. I could have sat in disappointment. I could have replayed every decision, every answer, every moment of the process, trying to explain the outcome. I could have called someone crying and asking why they didn't want me. I was grateful for the phone calls from educators and leaders across the country. But ambition that endures is ambition that adapts. I made a decision to let the setback serve as a catalyst, not a weight. I gave myself permission to step back from the outcome and sit inside a different, harder question: *What brings you joy?*

What Brings You Joy?

I lived with that question for five months. I carried it with me into every school I visited. I thought about it during long walks through buildings where students and teachers were creating the future, often without realizing it. I reflected on it during late evenings, during 5:00 a.m. gym workouts, revisiting what had shaped me, what had called me into leadership, what had sustained me in the hardest seasons of the work. That question pushed me to figure out who I wanted to be. The longer I lived in the question, the clearer my path became. Joy was built in the daily, sometimes invisible work of believing in people, believing in possibility, and believing in the power of service to change lives. The setback revealed a deeper ambition, one that was no longer contingent on circumstance. It asked me to let go of the need for immediate answers and to trust that the work I was meant to do would require me to grow in ways I had not yet seen. I took a setback and positioned it for a comeback.

Processing the setback was not about moving on quickly. It was about honoring the journey fully. It was about recognizing that personal and professional growth often happens in quiet spaces, where there is no audience, no applause, only the steady work of recommitting to the vision you carry for yourself. For me that was on a whiteboard at home. Sitting with the question *What brings you joy?* became a discipline in itself — a practice of listening to the deeper truths that ambition sometimes asks us to rediscover.

Letting go of something I loved was hard. February 28, 2023, marked my last day as Superintendent of Middletown City School District. I remember carrying one small brown box of items down to my truck. Yes, just one box. I spent the morning doing what had always brought me the deepest joy: walking through schools, connecting with people, celebrating the daily life of a community I loved. There was no grand event planned. No spotlight. Just the simple, powerful rhythm of a school day, the place where the real heart of a district lives. After a day of goodbyes, I had a scheduled end of the day school visit at Mayfield Elementary with Principal Keal. I made my way to Mayfield Elementary, one of our elementary schools filled with the kind of spirit that made #MiddieRising what it was. Getting out of the car, I found my heart pounding because I knew this was it. My last #MiddieRising experience.

I visited classrooms alongside Principal Keal, watching students engage in projects, lessons, and conversations that would shape the trajectory of their lives in ways they didn't even realize yet. I smiled, I listened, I soaked it in. Every corner of that building held memories. Like the water dunk tank for the end-of-year field day, reminders of how I always voted Mrs. Keal's office door last place for every door decorating contest, and my conversations with Mr. Manning in his Science class. As I walked the halls that day, I knew in my heart that my relationship with #MiddieRising was minutes away from closing. But knowing it intellectually was different than feeling it rise up in your chest, unexpected and heavy.

Toward the end of the visit, I observed students in one of the classes giving presentations. I sat quietly in the back of the room, squeezing my adult body into one of those tiny chairs built for elementary children. It felt good to be small again, to let the enormity of the moment shrink for just a few minutes. As I watched the students present, a little girl walked quietly toward me, clutching something in her hand. She reached me without a word, placed a small red piece of paper in my hand, and gave me a quick hug before turning back toward her classmates. This would be my last interaction with a MCSD student.

I looked down. She had cut a pink piece of paper into the shape of a heart, about the size of her hand. Written on it, in simple, unsteady handwriting, were five words: "I will miss you Mr. Styles."

The emotions of that heart hit harder than any speech, any ceremony, any announcement could have. I sat there, holding that small pink heart, feeling a rush of gratitude and heartbreak rise all at once. It was the moment I had been avoiding. The moment when love for a place meets the necessity of letting it go. Tears filled my eyes before I even realized they were coming. I bowed my head slightly, breathing in the truth that service to others, when done with heart, will always leave you grieving something you loved.

Driving away from Mayfield Elementary that afternoon, the emotions I had kept compartmentalized for over a year finally found their release. I cried as I pulled away from the school, tears falling silently in the car as I drove through the streets of a community that had shaped so much of who I had become. It was the kind of grief that only exists when something has mattered so much that leaving it feels like leaving a part of yourself behind. It was the confirmation that the work we had done together had been real, and that it had meant something lasting.

The little pink heart stayed with me that day–tucked safely into my bag, held quietly between moments of reflection. That small little pink heart captured the truth I had spent months trying to live inside: that joy is found in the impact you make when you lead with love and authenticity.

> That joy is found in the impact you make when you lead with love and authenticity.

Turning Setbacks Into Comebacks

In the months that followed, I carried that clarity into every new move I made. I had lived the question: *What brings you joy?* long enough to trust the answer. The setback from the CPS Superintendent interview had not diminished my belief or stole my confidence—it had refined it. It forced me to understand that sometimes the most powerful comeback is not about proving anything to anyone else. It is about rediscovering who you are, and choosing to move forward with everything you have become.

Navigating an ambitious journey will test you and reward you, often at the same time. There will be phases when the journey feels heavier than you imagined, when the obstacles feel closer than the opportunities. But there will also be moments of victory—moments when you realize you have grown stronger, wiser, and more resilient because you chose not to turn away from the harder road. Every step you have taken to build your belief system, to strengthen your ambition, and to center around your purpose has prepared you for the journey you have set for yourself.

You do not have to wonder if adversity will surface. It will. It is something every ambitious person has in common. We all encounter moments that test our commitment to the dreams we carry. Setbacks can deepen your resolve. They sharpen your understanding of what you truly value. They call you to rise, not by abandoning your aspirations, but by anchoring yourself even more firmly in them. Every person who has ever built something meaningful has faced a challenge along the way. What separates those who move with ambition is a mindset to use it as a bridge toward a stronger, more defined future.

> Setbacks will stretch you. So let them. They are a test to see how bad you want it.

Setbacks will stretch you. So let them. They are a test to see how bad you want it. At the start of the chapter, I invited you to draw your own lessons for how you'll choose to respond the next time you face a setback. Please take the time to do exactly that.

CHAPTER 5

Let Your Work Speak for Itself

The Weight of Expectation and the Work That Endures

There is a moment in every ambitious journey when a certain noise becomes the enemy of growth. Not external criticism, but the noise of comparison, of recognition-chasing, of pressure to prove yourself instead of preparing yourself. In that moment, something quietly courageous must take hold: a decision to anchor your energy on strategic execution, not external applause. This chapter encourages you to consider a certain mindset in these moments. For those seeking to step into a new role or expand their impact, the temptation is real: to equate progress with attention. In today's culture of optics, performance is often mistaken for motion, and validation becomes its own distorted reward system. Oftentimes the culture of expectations asks, "What did they see you do today?" Real elevation comes from how well you've positioned yourself through belief, discipline, strategy, and integrity. That's the kind of positioning you've been building since Chapter 1.

MAKE YOUR MOVE

Back in Chapter 1, you defined your ambition not as a chase for titles, but as a force driven by purpose, clarity, and internal alignment. You committed to a set of core principles: *Purpose, Vision, Bold Agency,* and *Disciplined Consistency.* These are the cornerstones for how you show up in pursuit of something meaningful. Chapter 5 is the test of that architecture. It's the moment when you keep doing the right work for the right reasons—even when the opportunity you've been working so hard for still has not presented itself.

So what happens when you're doing the work—and the opportunity doesn't come? When the recognition you hoped for goes to someone else? When your results are real but overlooked? There will be days when the ambitious grind feels routine, even taxing. There will be days where there is no spotlight or breakthrough. Just you, putting in the hard work, trying to make a move. On those days, it helps to focus on staying the course. You took this journey because something in you believed you were capable of more. Challenge yourself to stay true to the belief system you built and find a way to stay aligned to it. Take a moment and check in. How often are you showing up in your Fresh Styles? Those daily habits you chose back when your vision was clear? What milestones are you making progress on, even in small ways? Your Work Rate and Progress Pulse Checks serve as strategic reminders. They tell you whether the work you're doing is still connected to the future you're building. They give you something solid to stand on during periods when your motivation is running low. Invite yourself to keep honoring the reason you started this journey. Consider anchoring yourself in the Chapter 1, *Move with Ambition* definition that moves us forward:

> *To Move with Ambition is to find strength in the inspiration that lives in your heart, act decisively on what matters most, and stay deeply connected to your highest aspirations.*

For many, especially those rising in systems where visibility is currency, the pressure to be noticed is relentless. The demand to post, report, showcase, and amplify every step becomes its own form of labor. Somewhere along the way, the quality of the work gets traded for the optics of activity. The grind becomes noisy, and what was once driven by purpose begins to orbit around perception. This chapter offers a different way forward. It's an invitation to recommit to the kind of performance that doesn't require a spotlight to matter. It's a challenge to trust your cadence, your clarity, and your preparation long before the applause—or the absence of it—catches up. Remember that doing work rooted in belief and strategic execution speaks in outcomes, in trust, and in transformation.

Letting your work speak for itself requires belief in yourself. When your work speaks for itself, it demands a type of strategic maturity that can resist the urge to chase affirmation and instead commit to process, alignment, and discipline. When you learn to operate from this posture—when you build the system, refine the strategy, and prepare people—your impact becomes undeniable. To let your work speak for itself is to believe that legacy is louder than likes. It's to reject the short-term optics game in favor of long-game transformation. And in a culture that increasingly rewards immediacy, this decision is radical.

> To let your work speak for itself is to believe that legacy is louder than likes.

In this chapter, we'll explore how this philosophy has guided real transformational moments from quiet seasons of strategic alignment to years-long investments that ultimately yielded great opportunities. You'll encounter stories where work was done behind the scenes, yet its impact could be traced long after the meetings ended. You'll learn how to structure your work rhythm around what matters most: readiness, not recognition. And you'll gain a framework for operating with credibility and composure when no one is watching.

The next section will examine the temptation to be seen, the toll it takes, and the deeper transformational posture that allows us to exceed the culture of expectations by doing the work with a strategic purpose that endures.

Strategic Integrity Over External Optics

The professional world is increasingly shaped by the optics of performance. What's visible often carries more perceived value than what's vital. Schools and systems applaud polished presentations, elevated social media profiles, and the veneer of progress. But there's a deeper truth: work that transforms lives and systems rarely announces itself in real time. It unfolds in the steady cycle of preparation, strategy, and deeply aligned execution. The real work that positions us to be successful looks uneventful on the surface. It's time consuming, messy, and layered. And it rarely fits cleanly into a Tweet, a board presentation, or a newsletter. The temptation, however, is to *perform* our responsibilities rather than *embody* them. When the applause of optics begins to feel like progress, we risk detaching from the work that actually creates it.

> Work that transforms lives and systems rarely announces itself in real time. It unfolds in the steady cycle of preparation, strategy, and deeply aligned execution.

Here's what that detachment can look like: a leader who's busy managing impressions but avoiding hard decisions. A team that's so focused on publishing results that they neglect the culture needed to sustain them. A strategy that looks bold on the whiteboard, but lacks the infrastructure and human investment to survive first contact with implementation. Letting the work speak for itself begins with reclaiming integrity over image. It's a challenge to anchor your movement in something deeper than visibility. Strategic integrity is the internal commitment to do the right work even when it doesn't yield immediate recognition. It means measuring progress by alignment to vision. There's a maturity to this posture. It demands you ask harder questions of yourself and your team. Are we solving the right problems? Are we moving people toward meaningful change, or just managing expectations? Are we building capacity, or just building presentations?

You've likely felt this tension, especially if you're operating in systems where outcomes are politicized, where perception matters for professional survival, or where pressure to show results supersedes the time needed to do the right work and to do the work right. In those moments, letting the work speak for itself feels risky. But it's also where resilience is tested and revealed. Truly ambitious people build internal alignment so strong that when the time for recognition comes, the results speak louder than any pitch ever could.

Let me offer you a mental model here: think of your leadership like an iceberg. What people see (the public wins, the visible moves, the results in the data) is the tip. But what holds it up, what gives it weight and credibility, is everything beneath the surface. Your preparation. Your momentum markers. The conversations you've had that no one clapped for. The decisions you made to slow down when it would have been easier to sprint for approval. That's the grind. That's the integrity that allows the work to speak. Strategic integrity also protects you. It shields your decision-making from the emotional highs and lows of external affirmation. When you're anchored in clarity, you don't need the world to validate your every move. You know what you're building. You know what it's for. And you know the difference between popularity and progress.

Let's accept that this is a refinement of purpose. When we exceed the culture of expectations, we stop chasing performance for performance's sake. Instead, we build structures, teams, and systems that reflect our deepest commitments.

In the next section, we'll turn from this philosophy to something more personal. I'll share the story behind why I believe in this so deeply, and how that belief shaped the way I lead, move, and position myself to be successful.

Personal Philosophy of Execution

I've always believed in the power of doing the right work for the right reasons. It's never been about being seen or recognized. It's been about showing up for everyone I serve and everything I commit to. Consistently. Intentionally. Fully committed to doing my part to contribute to the culture and to the team. That mindset didn't come from a book or a leadership seminar, it came from lived experience. From years of navigating professional spaces where what got recognized wasn't always what created change. From watching systems reward visibility, while undervaluing depth. And from learning, sometimes the hard way, that lasting impact is rarely the impact that garners immediate celebration.

Early in my leadership journey, I decided that I wasn't going to spend my energy chasing validation from someone else. I was going to chase a reputation built on hard work. I was going to do the work that moved people and systems toward something better even if that work wasn't headline-ready. I didn't need the spotlight. I needed purpose. And that purpose became a code I carried with me: *keep your head down, do your work to the best of your ability, and let your work speak for itself.* During my time as assistant principal at Northwest High School, I recall teachers sharing that they wish they knew their schedules and student rosters before they left for the summer. At the same time, our administrative team and building leadership team had a number of creative ideas to reimagine the master schedule. I remember that year I was assigned the responsibility of creating the master schedule for the school. It was my first time ever doing it. For an entire month, I met individually with department chairs, counselors, small groups of students, and other assistant principals exploring strategies guided by our desired outcomes. I put my head down night after night, Saturday mornings, and early weekday mornings, trying every way possible to create a template that worked. I often challenged myself to make significant progress offline so the team had something positive to react to when we met again. Our building leadership team met monthly, so I would do my best to have a template to offer the team every time we met. Nobody required this from me, it was just important to me to work hard so that the team had something to react to that represented their most creative thoughts.

In late Spring of 2006, I delivered my first high school master schedule to the staff that consisted of interdisciplinary teams, common subject-based department planning, and a few more creative nuggets embedded in the schedule. In late May, teachers received their teaching assignments, counselors had access to a master schedule that ran ninety-plus percent accurate, and teachers had fairly accurate student rosters. We, the team, officially had a template that supported the strategic moves we were trying so hard to make to impact the student experience. At the time, all that hard work was purely to meet the needs of the most important people in the building. There was no standing ovation or employee-of-the-year award at the time for building the master schedule template, but all that hard work did build my confidence as a young leader. Two years later, the school saw significant improvement in student achievement scores. Staff members could be seen celebrating the big gains we made. I know there were a number of factors that contributed to our success: teachers caring for students, departments committing to collaboration, the leadership of the administrative team, and the hard work of the counseling department. But I was proud of the master schedule template I built that created space for each big move to show up and have a positive impact. I let my work speak for itself.

The truth is, letting the work speak for itself requires more from you. It asks you to live with delayed recognition and sometimes no recognition. To believe in results that may take years to mature. To persist in times where all your hard work takes place behind the scenes and nobody even knows how hard you are grinding. It became a behavior of mine to push through the hard stuff, keep my head down, and do my work for the right reasons. It became an all-of-the-time behavior for me. Not some of the time. I measured success not by whether people noticed, but by whether I knew the work was anchored in the collective purpose of the team. Was it aligned to our mission? Was it preparing people for what was next? Was it stretching our capacity to serve with excellence? Over time, it built a kind of credibility where people knew I always would show up prepared. That I would operate with integrity. That my decisions were grounded in strategy, not ego. That's what letting my work speak for itself eventually earned me: Trust.

But this part of my belief system was tested. There were times in my career when others advanced faster because they mastered the optics game. Parallel to the two-year story I just shared, is a story of other assistant principals in other buildings being celebrated for their leadership. I recall being at Central Office one day, and hearing a district administrator praise another assistant principal, stating that the leader would be a great fit for the next principal opening in the district. Man, did that sting! I had been working my tail off for two years as an aspiring principal trying to prepare myself for the next opportunity. It was a huge reality check to hear the comment from the district administrator because I felt my body of work was so strong. Maybe I wasn't playing the game the right way. This was the moment when I questioned whether staying rooted in execution was costing me the visibility I needed. Those doubts are real. And if you've ever wondered if it's worth it to stay the course while others perform their way to the next opportunity—you're not alone.

What I've come to learn is that ambition rooted in purpose will outlast ambition rooted in recognition. Because when the spotlight fades, and the metrics change, and the expectations shift, the people who were only performing lose their footing. But the ones who built from purpose? We don't miss a beat and we are always ready. Over my years of service in education, I have made it an everyday mindset to keep my head down and let my work speak for itself. During consultations, coaching calls, or interacting with educators in professional development spaces, I have encouraged others to do the same. To commit to preparing themselves and positioning themselves to be successful. Letting your work speak for itself means your effort is so disciplined, so aligned, and so real that it becomes undeniable. You don't have to announce it. All you have to do is just live it every single day.

> Ambition rooted in purpose will outlast ambition rooted in recognition.

In the next section, I'll take you into a story that shaped my understanding of what it means to lead with this mindset in high-stakes environments. It's about patience, preparation, and the belief that strategic work, done with conviction, can shape systems long before it's ever publicly acknowledged.

Ready Now 100: Planting Seeds for Future Impact

In the summer of 2021, I was part of a series of meetings that, at first glance, looked unremarkable. No one posted about them on any social media platform. Nobody from the local press or news was writing about what was being discussed in these meetings. As the Superintendent, I had no immediate data for the Board of Education to indicate the accomplishment of a particular milestone. But what happened during those months became one of the most defining examples in my leadership journey of what it truly means to let the work speak for itself.

In our strategic plan, we called it the *Ready Now 100* campaign, a commitment to prepare for a bold, strategic shift that wouldn't impact our students for years. Over the course of a five-year period, we were looking for one hundred endorsements of our Passport to Tomorrow (P2T). The Passport to Tomorrow is the district's strategic vision that helps students explore what they're interested in, set goals, and get ready for life after graduation. It provides students real-world experiences, shows them different career paths, and provides the tools they need to succeed in whatever path they choose. Endorsements would come from businesses, higher education institutions, and enlistment agencies in our region. The endorsement signaled a new reimagined partnership that consisted of a commitment to expose students to the different career fields and clusters, access to business facilities for onsite experiences, and human capital to inspire the young minds. The *Ready Now 100* campaign was built based on a deeply coordinated series of conversations, calibrating stakeholders on the vision, and system-level preparations designed to lay the groundwork for transforming student experiences through these new partnerships. The ultimate goal? To ensure that more students in our system had access to high-quality, career-aligned experiences that were endorsed by industry, valued by colleges, and meaningful to families. During the summer, I met with countless small groups of executives and owners building a shared understanding of what we were trying to do for students. A formal request for endorsement came at the end of the meetings, but often required follow up individual meetings to deeply explore how the new partnership could benefit the students.

The challenge? The real impact wouldn't be visible until long after the meetings ended. The decisions we were making—about partnerships, program design, and system readiness were seeds of opportunity. And I knew from the start: this wouldn't be work that got instant credit. It would be slow, technical, layered work. It would demand presence, precision, and a refusal to be distracted by the comments of others.

Every week that summer, we met with potential partners—community organizations, industry leaders, postsecondary institutions. They were working meetings, full of whiteboards, shared documents, hard questions, and creative friction. We were inspiring the region and building the credibility of the Passport to Tomorrow (P2T). I was in pursuit of one hundred endorsements, but started at zero. When the summer ended, I had only earned the district three endorsements. I am sure my team, the Board of Education, and the staff began doubting our ability to achieve one hundred endorsements. At times, it felt like we were moving through fog. The pressure to show progress to stakeholders was real. The desire to say, "Look what we've done," was real. But we resisted that desire–not because we lacked urgency, but because we respected the complexity of what we were trying to build.

I stayed resilient knowing that if we built this collection of partnerships, it would inspire some pretty amazing experiences for students during our P2T days. So I doubled down on strategy and the commitment to put my head down and grind. Yes, I made several course corrections to the plan and timeline, but I celebrated the momentum we were building as the school year progressed. We closed out in June of 2022 hitting the first-year metric for endorsements. The summer of 2021 laid the foundation for what became a systemwide shift. We celebrated new student pathways opened with community and industry endorsements that hadn't existed before. Students found themselves enrolled in programs that matched their passion and set them up for postsecondary success, for example the Early College Academy. The public saw the change. The Middletown Police Department provided amazing career exploration experiences for students on our P2T days. I remember one day students learning about crime scene investigation and the careers in this area. Another time the officers brought technology resources used in law enforcement. The students loved the drones.

Nobody saw the countless blue blocks of P2T meetings on my Google calendar. They didn't know the ongoing conversations with Rick Pears from the Middletown Chamber of Commerce. The collaboration with him was monumental in the *Ready Now 100* campaign. I recall a nearby district celebrating the high number of business partners they had and the routine business partner luncheons they had. Again, the optics of what was happening in that district never became a distraction for us. Our strategy inspired the work we did. I found joy knowing all our hard work to grow the *Ready Now 100* was fueled by purpose and had a profound impact on every student in our system. The work spoke for itself and represented a new student-centered business partnership. I was proud of that. The lessons I carried forward from that experience were simple, but profound:

1. **Long-game leadership requires short-term humility.** You must be willing to move through seasons when the outcomes aren't obvious and the recognition might be non-existent.
2. **Systemic transformation starts in the quiet.** Public shifts are always preceded by private alignment. The most

meaningful change is born in meetings that nobody will celebrate publicly.
3. **Letting the work speak for itself requires relational equity.** The only reason those endorsements came through two years later is because of the trust we built in the early, invisible stages. A high value was placed on growing relationships with the goal that partners would find inspiration in our invitation to serve the youth.

There is something deeply liberating about operating this way. When you detach from the need to prove and instead focus on the need to prepare, your work takes on a new depth. It becomes about service, not spotlight. It becomes about stewardship of your time, your vision, and your people. *Ready Now 100* was never about doing something impressive. It was about doing something important. And that distinction matters. One feeds the ego. The other feeds the dreams of the people.

As we transition into the next section, I want to elevate this truth: strategic readiness is the most underrated form of an ambitious mindset in today's culture of urgency. If you can stay committed to building something very well, you'll create conditions others will thrive in long after you're gone. There was a period in my own leadership journey when I had to learn what it really means to do the right work without chasing recognition. A stretch where I learned to let my work speak for itself.

There's a temptation in education to treat each school year as a stand-alone sprint, an isolated push toward improvement, outcomes, and growth. When I served as superintendent, I learned that the most effective way to lead ambitious change wasn't through force or fanfare, so I had to discover an approach that invited our big ideas to come to light. Our team worked in cycles–intentional, disciplined cycles–that aligned our work to what the system was actually ready for. That cadence allowed us to exceed expectations without disrupting the culture the staff worked so hard to build. It gave our work structure. It gave our team shared ownership. And it allowed the work to position the district to be successful.

Our leadership year started not in the fall, but in the winter. From January to February, my executive team and I engaged in what we called our "Strategic Mapping" process. We would go off-site for two days for our own executive retreat to prepare for the following school year. This was rigorous, focused alignment on the pillars in our strategic plan. We asked ourselves: What are the most important moves we need to make next year? What systems need to be redesigned? What opportunities must we pursue now to ensure we will be ready come the start of the school year? This period of time was about naming the ambition and looking at our students, our community, our culture and asking, "What are we uniquely positioned to do next?"

We would then spend March through April strategically planning for the next year. It's where we built the operational backbone of the strategy, defined the priorities, set the metrics, and clarified the roles and responsibilities. But more than anything, it was about people. We planned how to build capacity in principals, departments, and support teams to lead the work that lay ahead of us.

From April through early June, we did the best we could to build shared understanding. This might include dedicating time on the schedule to visit staff meetings at every building in the district to deliver a short presentation about what we hoped to accomplish the next school year. We consistently used our June end-of-year Leadership Retreat to set the stage for the next school year with every leader in the district. I enjoyed feeling that we had calibrated the staff to the best of our ability and offered inspiration on the exciting moves for the next school year.

My favorite part of the process was the period between August to December. Why? As focused as we were on execution and implementation of what we had planned, my interest was on something different. As much as I enjoyed being visible across the buildings, one of my goals for visiting schools was to maintain a clear sense of what the staff was excited about and what the system was ready for. I was addicted to gathering insight and information at all times. I needed to have a very clear understanding so that I could initiate a strategic planning process again that celebrated the impact of what was being accomplished. I had a number of strategies that helped me gauge readiness. For example, I conducted informal pulse checks with staff. Their insights allowed me to keep the pulse on what inspired them and their readiness for the next big implementation phase.

I'll be honest: it took time to develop this approach. In my early years as a leader, I felt reactive. I was in a cadence of being reactive, and not in tune to proactive initiatives. This pattern of behavior and practice led to misalignment, burnout, and inconsistent outcomes. Just because something is important doesn't mean you're ready to do it well. And just because something feels slow doesn't mean it isn't strategic.

When I shifted from reactive urgency to an intentional strategic cadence, outcomes changed. Our cultures changed for the better. Our leaders began to trust that they didn't have to sprint every day to be effective. The work we were doing started to become fun.

Imagine the number of meetings, walkthroughs, conversations, and planning sessions that took place to execute this strategic approach. You won't find a social media post celebrating a hallway conversation with a staff member or any other recognition-based scenario. As a team, we just put our heads down and did the necessary work to set us up for success. The lesson I want to leave with you here is this: a strategic and disciplined cadence to how you go about doing your work influences its impact. There is no need to rush; there is reward in being methodical and hard working.

Call to Action and Reflection Prompts

At this point, the question isn't whether the quiet grind matters. It's whether you're willing to live it. Whether you're ready to trust and prioritize preparation over performance. Whether you're serious enough about your goals to work to achieve them without the potential for recognition. To exceed the culture of expectations not by rising above it for attention, but by going deeper than it ever demanded.

Letting your work speak for itself is a declaration of who you are. It's a disciplined, internal commitment to outcomes that aren't dependent on applause. And it's a rejection of the lie that your value is proven by how loudly or frequently you're seen. It is evidence that you are making progress toward the momentum milestones you have set for that big move you ambitiously want to make. But make no mistake: this is not easy work. The quiet grind tests your patience. You'll be tempted to chase immediacy and forget your strategy. To sacrifice your aspirations. That's why this mindset requires reflection because no one else will hold you accountable for staying in alignment with your purpose but you. Here are a few questions to sit with as you integrate this chapter's message into your practice:

Reflection Prompts

- Where in your current work are you trading visibility for depth?
- Are your daily actions aligned with the momentum milestones you've set, or are you managing optics?

LET YOUR WORK SPEAK FOR ITSELF

- When was the last time you paused to prepare, instead of pushing forward out of urgency?
- What systems are you building now that won't speak until years from now? And are you at peace with that timeline?
- Do your habits reflect belief in your vision—or a need for validation?

The truth is, not everyone around you will understand your grind. Some will question it. Others will overlook the depth. But if your work is rooted in purpose, sustained by a disciplined approach, and carried out with credibility—it will speak for itself. And when it does, it will speak louder than any title, louder than any recognition, and louder than any temporary applause.

So here is your charge: Stop working to be noticed. Start working so your impact can't be ignored. Protect the joy you have for what you do. Let your credibility speak in outcomes, not optics. When all is said and done, successful ambitious people are remembered for what they left behind. The culture of expectations will always chase the visible, the immediate, the now. But your greatest work will live in the systems you build, the impact of your work, the people you develop, and the outcomes that echo long after you've left the room.

So grind on—strategically, purposefully, unapologetically. And when doubt creeps in, because it will, be sure to remind yourself to have the confidence knowing your efforts won't just say what you've done. They will show who you've become.

CHAPTER 6

Stepping Into the Right Fit

When you've been building toward something for a long time, every opportunity can start to feel like the one you've been preparing for. The best part of the journey is when you find yourself face to face with an opportunity to advance or take on a new role. At this stage, the most important question becomes whether the opportunity is a match for who you are becoming. This chapter brings you into that moment when you are trying to decide if you should pursue or take advantage of the opportunity presenting itself. Whether the opportunity found you or you actively pursued it, you're now standing at the edge of decision. What comes next will influence your energy, your growth, and your ability to lead in alignment with your ambitions.

Fit signals congruence—between your preparation, your identity, and your ambition. It connects deeply to how you show up and how you sustain yourself in the work. It draws on the belief you've built and the integrity you've protected. Fit invites you to engage with discernment, not impulse, and to move with alignment. Many people reach this phase with a sense of anticipation. The role looks meaningful. The environment appears promising. Yet the next step depends on a deeper layer of reflection. You're being asked to assess the opportunity based on how well it supports the person you are and the purpose you've named. The questions now become clearer: *Does this allow me to lead with conviction? Does this move align with the long-term contribution I've committed to make? Will I remain grounded and recognizable to myself as I step into what's next?*

To engage with those questions, this chapter brings forward three real experiences. Each one offers insight into how fit is revealed through action and awareness. One person discovers a shift in their path that brings them into closer connection with their sense of purpose. Another finds that a long-awaited role introduces unexpected tension with the values they hold. A third enters a leadership position with full alignment between identity and opportunity and experiences growth and fulfillment as a result. These stories are accompanied by a core lesson, a reflection on why it matters, and a set of considerations to help you examine your own experiences. They represent the lived process of engaging ambition with maturity. Each story adds dimension to what it means to move forward with clarity. This part of the journey is not about whether you say yes or no. It's about the lens you use to interpret the choices in front of you and the way you decide where and how to apply your capacity. These stories are offered as reflections to guide your discernment. They give shape to the process of evaluating fit through identity, discipline, and vision.

As you move through the lessons, consider what you've learned from the experiences that shaped you. Look at the patterns in your past that revealed positive energy or resistance. Pay attention to what remains true in your decision-making and what has evolved. When fit is aligned with purpose, your habits hold steady. Your energy has direction. And your ambition matures with focus. Let's begin with the first lesson.

Lesson 1: Same Purpose—A Shift in the Path Forward

She was born with a helper's heart. From the time she was a teenager growing up in Michigan, she found herself drawn to situations where care and recovery were needed. In high school, she spent hours volunteering in the athletic training room. She showed up for practices, stayed late during competitions, and never hesitated when someone needed ice, tape, or just a quiet voice to say, "You're going to be OK." There was something about the way she moved in those spaces—focused, present, invested. By the time she entered her senior year, she had secured an internship at a local medical facility, shadowing physical therapists and absorbing everything she could about the profession. It wasn't a career fantasy. It was an ambition that had already begun taking shape. She wanted to be a physical therapist when she graduated.

She entered college with a great deal of excitement about her future. With each class she took, her interest became more precise. What fascinated her wasn't just anatomy or injury response—it was the problem-solving. She was wired to notice where someone was struggling, understand the pain behind the limitation, and build a plan that led to healing. Her ambition was inspired by getting people back on their feet. What mattered most was making someone feel better, stronger, and more capable than they did the day before. Her professors saw her potential. She excelled in coursework and connected easily with peers. Every signal said she was on the right path. When the time came to begin field placements, she approached it with excitement. The placement site was a mid-sized rehabilitation facility with a steady flow of patients. From day one, she tried to pour herself into the work. She greeted each patient warmly, observed carefully, and participated in any way the supervising staff allowed. Her natural energy made her a fast favorite among some of the patients. She felt the work clicking in real time. Each day brought new insights, new techniques, and new opportunities to serve. This, she thought, is what fit is supposed to feel like. But not everyone saw it the same way.

Several weeks into the placement, a supervising physical therapist pulled her aside for a conversation. It was framed as a casual check-in, a quick discussion about how she was adjusting to the work. She was prepared to share her growth, her reflections, her sense of purpose. Instead, what she heard would unsettle her entire sense of direction.

"I want to share something that might be hard to hear," the supervisor began. "You bring a lot of positivity to the room. But I've been watching closely, and I must be honest. It doesn't seem like you fit. You're not doing anything wrong. But something about the way you move through this space just doesn't feel like you're meant to be a physical therapist."

The conversation didn't last much longer. The words weren't angry or loud. But they cut deep. *You don't fit.* Not because of a missed assignment or poor interaction. Not because of attitude or lack of effort. Simply because, in the supervisor's opinion, she didn't carry the intangible essence of someone who belonged in that profession.

She left the facility that day in silence. The phrase echoed in her mind—*you don't fit*—and challenged every assumption she had carried into that placement. For years, she had believed this was her path. She had built her education around it. She had pursued opportunities to deepen her understanding and refine her skill. Now someone inside the field was telling her it didn't feel right. That word—*fit*—landed like a riddle she couldn't quite solve.

Later that night, sitting in her dorm room, she allowed the weight of the moment to settle. The sadness came first. Then the confusion. Then, something else: clarity. She thought carefully about what had driven her this far. It wasn't the title of physical therapist. It was the desire to help people heal, to guide them forward, to meet them in a moment of need and make that moment better. Within two weeks, she was seated in her academic advisor's office. Junior year. Halfway through her program. She had made her decision. She was switching majors. The choice: Education.

She was deciding to reframe her dream. She was still going to help people heal. Still going to support their growth. Still going to bring her energy, her problem-solving, and her belief in others to the table. But instead of a rehabilitation center, it would be a classroom. She graduated with a degree in middle grades education. Her first job was in a public middle school not far from her hometown. On the first day, standing in front of a room full of students, she felt something she hadn't experienced in a long time: peace. This was her space. These were her people. She had found the place where her passion, her energy, and her skill aligned. Over the next fifteen years, she taught, led, and grew. She became a middle school principal. Later, she transitioned into district leadership. Each role allowed her to make an impact—not by fitting someone else's mold, but by stepping into the space where she could thrive.

What changed her life was the reflection that followed the setback. Fit is about recognizing when something doesn't align, and having the courage to redirect before your ambition is trapped in someone else's version of success. She realigned her dream. And in doing so, she found her perfect fit.

+ **Why It Matters**
  Alignment is not always revealed at the beginning of the journey. Sometimes it becomes clear through lived experience. When a shift in direction occurs, the core purpose can remain strong while the path evolves to better support it. This kind of realignment honors both the work you've done and the clarity you've gained.

Consider
>What insights—formal or informal—have helped clarify where you do your best work? Is there a moment, either in your past or leading up to a recent opportunity, that was difficult to accept at the time but ultimately brought you closer to a more authentic expression of your purpose?

Lesson 2: Reality Check–A Desire for a Better Fit

Not long ago, I had a conversation with a school leader in Ohio who had just finished their first year in a new administrative role. We had known each other for a while, crossed paths at conferences, exchanged messages now and then, and when we finally sat down to talk, I could tell they were carrying something heavy. They had taken a building-level leadership job with the kind of optimism you'd expect from someone stepping into a dream they had chased for years. But one year in, the dream didn't feel like a dream anymore. They had done everything you're supposed to do. Joined committees. Led projects. Built relationships across the district. Earned their administrative license while balancing full-time work and full-time life. They had checked every box. Not out of obligation, but out of deep, real ambition. They believed leadership was the next right move. But now, sitting across from me, they said the words that stopped me cold: "This job is not what I thought it was going to be."

There was complete and authentic honesty in the tone and position. They went on to describe their experience in detail, not to complain, but to reflect. The paperwork. The meetings. The evening obligations. The long hours away from their family. The constant stream of directives from the central office, each one urgent, each one layered on top of the last. But what hit hardest was this: "I miss being in the classroom. I miss being with kids. I don't get to do that anymore. I spend more time reacting to problems than creating momentum." It was a simple truth, rising to the surface after twelve months of doing the work: the job didn't align with who they were becoming. That moment deserves our full attention.

This was someone who had positioned themselves for success with strategy, discipline, and a heart full of purpose. They had visualized the move and prepared for it with care. They had stepped forward with courage. But even after all of that, after making all the right moves, the opportunity turned out not to be the right fit. And that realization shook them. Because what do you do when the door you worked so hard to open leads to a room that doesn't feel like yours? There's a deeper lesson here, and it has nothing to do with whether the job was hard or whether the leader was talented. The lesson is this: readiness does not guarantee alignment. And effort, even when it's extraordinary, does not always equal fit.

Too often, we treat opportunity like it's always a gift. Like saying "Yes" is automatically the right move if we've done the work to earn the chance. But every opportunity has a reality. And if that shape doesn't match your values, your energy, and your long-term vision, then what looks like a step forward can end up pulling you away from the very purpose that brought you here. Let's pause here and imagine something different.

What if, before accepting the role, this leader had taken a full step back, not to question their ambition, but to evaluate the opportunity with more clarity? What if they had asked not just *Can I do this job?* But *will this job allow me to live out my purpose?* What if they had examined the work not just from the lens of leadership, but from the lens of alignment? Would they have made the same move? Would they have saved themselves from months of resume updates, job board searches, and interview cycles? Would they have protected themselves from the emotional toll of self-doubt that so often creeps in when a door we fought to open ends up feeling like a misstep? I just want to emphasize that my focus is not on regret, but on honest reflection.

This chapter has made one truth clear: not every opportunity is meant for you. And the more aspirational your goals become, the more essential it is to slow down before you say yes. Especially when the opportunity sounds like a dream. Especially when everyone else sees it as a win. Because nobody else has to live your purpose. You do. That's the key challenge underneath all this. We must learn how to evaluate opportunities not from a place of ego or urgency, but from a place of alignment to our purpose. We must ask harder questions. Not, *Will this look good on my resume?* But, *Will this allow me to thrive?* Not, *Will this make me look more successful?* But, *Will this fill my cup?*

The leader I spoke with is still on their journey. And while this year wasn't what they hoped it would be, it gave them something even more valuable than affirmation: it gave them clarity. Clarity about what matters most to them. Clarity about what kind of leader they want to be. Clarity about how they want to show up for kids, for staff, and for themselves. So before you step into the next role, the next title, the next bold move—pause. Look closer. Go deeper. Ask the questions only you can answer. Don't just position yourself for the opportunity. Position the opportunity within your purpose so you can be excited about it being the right fit.

- **Why It Matters**
  Sometimes, fit is revealed through lived experience. The daily patterns of a role can teach you more about yourself than any job description. When you reflect on what isn't working or what doesn't feel right, you gain clarity about what will help you grow. Dreams can be reshaped and plans can change.

- **Consider**
  What have you learned about yourself from a role that didn't feel quite right? How do you want to feel in your next opportunity, not just in terms of outcome, but in daily experience?

Lesson 3: Thriving–The Opportunity Fit My Purpose

Every so often, I get the chance to watch someone step into the right role and come fully alive in it because they did the internal work to make sure the move was right. When these kinds of moments happen, they give me goosebumps. You can feel it when it happens—when someone makes a move and everything about it clicks. Passion. Joy. Service. Authenticity. Watching someone thrive like that, right out of the gate, is one of the great privileges of this work.

I want to tell you about my friend Neil Gupta. He is one of the most thoughtful and values-driven leaders I've ever had the privilege of knowing. He's spent years contributing to the field of education with sincerity, service, and a deep sense of purpose. When he began considering the superintendency at Oakwood City Schools in Ohio, it was immediately clear it was something for which he had been quietly preparing for a long time. We talked throughout the process, and it was through those brief check-ins that I knew he was on the cusp of something meaningful. He had taken the time to study the district, to listen carefully to what the community was asking for, and to look honestly at who he was and what he had to offer. Neil never mentioned his desire to be the superintendent, although it was implied. He wanted to lead in a place where his purpose, his vision for the youth, and the district's direction could align. It was like watching someone play matchmaker—not between people, but between identity and opportunity.

Neil could articulate, without notes, why this role was the right fit for him. "I've been working on this type of strategic planning for the last few years," he told me. "They're looking for someone who can lead that work. I know the community values high expectations and a personal touch, and I thrive in that space." As he spoke, you could feel the alignment based on the audit he had already done ahead of his decision.

When Neil accepted the role and became superintendent of Oakwood, what happened only affirmed what was already true before he took the seat. In his first year, Neil absolutely thrived. The district moved forward with a clear vision for the future. The community was engaged. Exciting initiatives gained traction, and the community celebrated the great work of the staff. And perhaps the most important thing about the story? Neil was still Neil. He did not need to change who he is to succeed in the role. He hasn't had to contort his leadership style or abandon his values to meet someone else's expectations. The same habits that shaped him before are the same habits sustaining him in the move now. That's what I want you to take away from Neil's story.

When you take time to align your purpose with an opportunity, you don't have to guess your way into getting ready for it. Neil didn't *hope* the role would fit him once he got there. He evaluated it in advance. He asked better questions of himself. He made sure the work he was walking into matched the values he was bringing with him. That's not just strategy. That's self-respect.

Second, your habits will either prepare you for the opportunity or expose the gap. Neil didn't change who he was to fit the seat. He brought the same disciplined consistency that had guided him before. Instead of scrambling to rise to the role, he stepped into it already grounded. The joy he feels now is the result of years of practicing what he believed in, long before his opportunity presented itself.

STEPPING INTO THE RIGHT FIT

This is what thriving looks like—not just success, but sustainable alignment to your purpose. A role that doesn't just challenge you, but affirms you. A seat that demands more from you, but never asks you to be less of yourself. That only happens when you make the match on purpose, with purpose. Neil didn't wait for the position to prove he was ready. He prepared like someone who knew what he was called to do. And now, the community he serves is better for it.

So here's the charge: Don't chase the role. Clarify your purpose. Don't guess your way into a job and hope it works out. Play matchmaker. Because when the fit is right and your habits are strong, you will come alive in the opportunity.

- **Why It Matters**
  When your habits and identity align with the opportunity in front of you, your energy becomes focused, and your contribution expands. Fit rewards the congruence between your preparation and the work you're being asked to do. The alignment between these serves as a retention mechanism in what brings you joy.

> When your habits and identity align with the opportunity in front of you, your energy becomes focused, and your contribution expands.

- **Consider**
  What aspects of you do you want to fully carry into your next opportunity? What type of role allows you to move without compromise—to thrive while staying grounded in your purpose?

Stretch Prompt: Identity and Opportunity Map

Create a two-column map. In the first column, list what defines you when you are at your best—your habits, your energy, your values, and the environments that bring out your strengths. In the second column, outline the conditions and demands of the next opportunity you're considering or preparing for. Study both sides. Where do you see alignment? Where do you notice potential strain? Use this map not just to evaluate the role, but to clarify what it will take to move with integrity and momentum.

How the Lessons Connect with Your Journey Thus Far

These three lessons are built on the foundation of the work you've already done in the earlier chapters of this book. Each one ties directly to the principles, mindset, and preparation you've been putting into place.

- **Lesson 1: Same Purpose–A Shift in the Path Forward:** This lesson carries a strong tie to the work you began in Chapter 1, especially around vision and purpose. The story highlights how ambition, when paired with self-awareness, can reveal new directions that still honor the original intent. The identity work from Chapter 2 also threads through here. Belief does not always mean staying fixed to one form—it means staying honest about what you're learning and how your sense of contribution is evolving. There's a subtle but important connection to Chapter 3 as well, where you started noticing how environments shape behavior. The shift in direction, in this case, emerged not from doubt, but from clear-eyed observation about where your gifts show up strongest.

- **Lesson 2: Reality Check–A Desire for a Better Fit:** This lesson reflects what you've built through disciplined consistency, one of the four key principles introduced early in the book. It also draws from the work you did in Chapter 3, where you learned to evaluate momentum—not just by pace or progress, but by the quality of the experience and how aligned it feels with your values. This story also bridges into Chapter 4, where navigating complexity requires staying anchored to your core. The leader in this example didn't lack drive or skill. They were navigating the tension that comes when external progress doesn't match internal alignment. That experience adds depth to the concept of fit and the importance of honest evaluation before making your next move.
- **Lesson 3: Thriving–The Opportunity Fits My Purpose:** This final lesson is a full-circle example of what happens when belief, identity, and preparation converge. You can trace this moment all the way back to Chapter 2, where you began refining your sense of belief—not as wishful thinking, but as a grounded understanding of what matters most to you. It also reflects the disciplined patterns you worked on in Chapter 1 and the aligned action you focused on in Chapter 3. When all those pieces come together—belief, preparation, rhythm, and clarity—you move into opportunities with confidence. This story models what alignment looks like when purpose leads and habits carry forward without disruption.

Each of these lessons builds on the thinking and habits you've already been shaping. The stories show different outcomes, but the through-line remains consistent: clarity, alignment, and growth. These are part of the larger arc of ambitious movement. And now that you've seen how these lessons emerge in real-world decisions, you're ready to move forward with even greater intention as you consider that next opportunity.

Bridging Reflection to Decision

The stories shared in this chapter offer more than insight—they offer a framework for seeing opportunity through the lens of alignment. Each experience reveals how people moved forward with clarity built from reflection, preparation, and conviction. The idea of fit becomes tangible when it's viewed not as a reward to chase, but as a relationship between readiness, identity, and contribution. As you close this section, the focus turns inward. You've been observing how others navigated pivotal decisions. Now it's time to evaluate what's in front of you with the same level of depth and intention. The role you are considering, the environment you are entering, the people you'll serve—these decisions require more than instinct. They ask for clarity grounded in your own work.

The next tool in this journey is built to support that clarity. The *Opportunity Alignment Assessment Tool* is a guided assessment that surfaces alignment between your ambition and the opportunity in view. Each reflection point connects back to core ideas you've already explored—your purpose, belief, habits, and highest aspirations. Approach this tool with honesty. Use your own words. Ground your responses in what you know to be true about yourself. This is the moment to evaluate what's emerging with the seriousness your future deserves.

Opportunity Alignment Assessment Tool: Is This the Right Fit?

Purpose of the Tool:

Use this tool to evaluate whether an opportunity truly aligns with your Ambitious Move. Reflect deeply, write honestly, and let your responses guide a thoughtful decision about what comes next. Each section integrates insights from your belief, purpose, habits, and ambition.

1. **The Opportunity**

    - Name or Description of Opportunity:

      _____

    - Brief Summary of What This Opportunity Entails:

      _____

      _____

      _____

      _____

2. **Alignment with Your Ambitious Move**
   → **Refer to Chapter 1: The Four Key Principles of Ambitious Movement**

    - What is your defined Ambitious Move?

      _____

      _____

      _____

    - Does this opportunity align with that vision?
      ☐ Yes ☐ No ☐ Unsure

- Why or why not?

   _____
   _____
   _____
   _____

3. **Purpose & Contribution**
   → **Refer to Chapter 1: Define Move with Ambition**

   - How does this opportunity connect to your deeper purpose?

     _____
     _____
     _____
     _____

   - What impact does it allow you to make beyond yourself?

     _____
     _____
     _____
     _____

- Score (1-4): Alignment with Purpose
  ☐ 1 – Misaligned   ☐ 2 – Surface-level connection
  ☐ 3 – Mostly aligned   ☐ 4 – Deeply aligned with my mission

4. **Belief Identity & Self-Awareness**
   → **Refer to Chapter 2: Coming Together with Your Belief + Creating the Way Forward with Commitment**

   - What core belief(s) from your Belief Blueprint are relevant here?

   _____

   _____

   _____

   - Does this opportunity affirm or challenge your sense of identity?

   _____

   _____

   _____

   - Score (1-4): Identity Alignment
     ☐ 1 – Not aligned   ☐ 2 – Minimal connection
     ☐ 3 – Partial fit   ☐ 4 – Strong alignment with who I am becoming

5. **Habits & Fresh Styles in Motion**
   → **Refer to Chapter 1: Fresh Habits + Chapter 3: Work Rate & Contribution Rate**

   - Which of your Fresh Styles will this opportunity strengthen or require?

   _____

   _____

   _____

   - What evidence can you provide that your daily habits position you well for this opportunity?

   _____

   _____

   _____

   _____

   - Score (1-4): Alignment with Daily Habits
     - ☐ 1 – Not supported by current habits
     - ☐ 2 – Requires major habit change
     - ☐ 3 – Supports growth of current habits
     - ☐ 4 – Strong fit with daily disciplines already in motion

6. **Fit with the Definition that Moves Us Forward**
   → **Refer to Chapter 1: Define Move with Ambition + Chapter 5: Quiet Power of Doing the Work**
   Definition: To *Move with Ambition* is to find strength in the inspiration that lives in your heart, act decisively on what matters most, and stay deeply connected to your highest aspirations.

   - **Inspiration from the Heart:**
     ✎ Does this opportunity align with what emotionally drives you?
     ☐ Yes   ☐ No   ☐ Partially
     ✎ Reflect:

     _____

     _____

     _____

   - **Acting on What Matters Most:**
     ✎ Will this allow you to act with clarity and conviction on what truly matters to you?
     ☐ Yes   ☐ No   ☐ Partially
     ✎ Reflect:

     _____

     _____

     _____

- **Connection to Highest Aspirations:**
  ✍ Does this move align with your long-term vision for impact and legacy?
  ☐ Yes ☐ No ☐ Partially
  ✍ Reflect:

  _____

  _____

  _____

- **Score (1-4): Fit with Move with Ambition Definition**
  ☐ 1 – Misaligned on all fronts
  ☐ 2 – Connected only at surface level
  ☐ 3 – Mostly aligned with 2 of 3 components
  ☐ 4 – Fully embodies all 3 elements

7. **Readiness to Thrive**
   → Refer to Chapter 4: Navigating the Ambitious Journey

   - **Will this opportunity allow you to thrive professionally, emotionally, and intellectually?**

   _____

   _____

   _____

   _____

- What conditions for thriving are present or missing?

  _____

  _____

  _____

  _____

- Score (1-4): Capacity to Thrive
  - ☐ 1 – Harmful to my well-being
  - ☐ 2 – Risky or uncertain
  - ☐ 3 – Supportive of growth
  - ☐ 4 – A clear environment where I can thrive

8. **Position Statement**
   → Refer to Chapter 6: Stepping Into the Right Fit
   After reflecting on all components, where do you stand?

Write your final decision about this opportunity and why you've made it. Be bold, be clear, be honest.

_____

_____

_____

_____

_____

Closing the Chapter: Make Your Move

This stage of the journey brings more than reflection. It brings responsibility, and asks you to stand fully inside your belief and decide what to do next with what you now know. Every question you've answered, every score you've given, and every insight you've surfaced has prepared you to do one thing: make your move.

Not every door will open. Not every opportunity will take shape the way you imagined. But that's not the measure of your ambition. When you make your move, you're stepping into something considered, earned, and built with intention. Believe that your time will come and the right opportunity will find its way to you. When it does, will you be ready to make the decision to act on it? If this opportunity becomes real, step into it fully. Own the moment. Show up with the belief and integrity you've cultivated through every chapter. And if it doesn't come to pass, keep your head up and stay rooted. Give your ambition permission to evolve over time.

CHAPTER 7

Living the Move

No one told me the hardest part wouldn't be getting the opportunity. It would be finding my footing once I got there. For years, I believed the biggest challenge would be positioning myself to be successful. I poured every ounce of energy into getting myself ready—earning trust, sharpening my craft, staying focused when it would've been easier to coast. I waited for the opportunity that felt like the right fit, one that would allow me to move in a way that matched my values and my ambition. And when that moment finally came, I stepped into it with a great deal of pride. I was confident I had earned my place. What I didn't expect was the required internal shift that would follow. Getting the job wasn't the hard part. Living in the move—that was the reality check that I did not expect. So I want to focus your mind and heart on preparing to live in the move.

My third year teaching demanded more of me than I had ever anticipated. And to be clear, I loved that year. I still hold deep appreciation for that part of my professional life. But it tested my capacity in ways that preparation alone couldn't predict. I had earned the opportunity to be in the professional role, but initially living in that role did not yet reflect a fully-formed identity. I had so much to learn, not just about the work, but about who I would need to become if I truly wanted to thrive.

I remember a moment that felt small at the time but changed the way I approached my classroom. One of my students raised his hand and said, "Mr. Styles, these worksheets are boring." He wasn't trying to be disrespectful—he was just being honest. It was a reality check that said, "Congratulations on achieving your goal, but you need to find a way to get better now that you are in it." That weekend, I found myself walking through grocery store aisles, jotting down prices, doing unit conversions, and building a real-world math lesson. The following week, I turned my classroom into a grocery store simulation where students went shopping during math class. Students had to calculate cost per ounce to find the best deals. They were engaged. Focused. Curious. That moment taught me something vital: creativity in the role was a professional obligation. I couldn't rely on the methods I'd inherited from my prep program in college. I had to become a designer of experiences. If I wanted students to fall in love with math, I needed to meet them at the intersection of relevance and rigor.

> **If I wanted students to fall in love with math, I needed to meet them at the intersection of relevance and rigor.**

That same year, I came to understand the real meaning of team. In the Introduction, I talked about my colleagues who pushed me, supported me, and helped shape my professional identity. Being part of that team showed me what it looks like to contribute inside a shared vision. It taught me to value collaboration not as a formality, but as a force multiplier. What we built together helped me realize that living inside my move was not a solo adventure. I could grow faster, lead stronger, and stay grounded when my contributions matched those of my teammates. That year shaped my understanding of what was possible when a team aligns around ambition.

But growth-provoking experiences weren't always affirming. I had to confront moments of uncertainty early on. During one observation in the early 2000s, I attempted a tech-integrated lesson—something new for me at the time. I gotta tell you that my lesson plan idea was solid. How I executed it was well below what the students deserved. Technical difficulties disrupted the flow. The students were confused. The lesson was a complete bust. My post-observation feedback was very direct, and I had to take responsibility for my failures. I was held accountable for what didn't work, and it stung. I remember sitting with that disappointment, questioning whether I could actually be great at this. That moment caused a great deal of deep reflection. But it's one of the reasons I became a stronger educator. I stopped avoiding feedback. I began seeking it. I realized that being held accountable was a gift. That's when I understood that growth can be fueled by the courage to get better.

There was also a deeper lesson brewing—one that didn't fully surface until years later. I had worked so hard to earn the role that I hadn't taken time to define what kind of teacher I wanted to be. My early focus was on proving I belonged. What I neglected was the work of clarifying what success actually looked like for me. Who I wanted to become? What did I want my students to feel in my presence? What would my classroom reflect about my beliefs? It took three years of living in the role before I had the clarity to answer those questions. That phase taught me the difference between having a title and building an identity.

And that's what I want you to reflect on here: not just the opportunity you are about to earn, but who you want to become as you live in your ambitious move.

Maybe you're reading this chapter after accepting a new role. Maybe you just got promoted. Maybe you transitioned industries or finally stepped into a space you've long aspired to enter. You prepared and planned for this. You showed up with credentials, character, and ambition. But once you begin living in the new move, something might feel off. You might find yourself navigating new expectations, new relationships, new systems. It's not that you're unqualified. It's that your new reality will be different. And your instincts might inform you that your new context demands more of you in the form of a new identity.

This is the tension no one really prepares you for: Consider the need to recalibrate your ambition while living in the move. That's the paradox of the move. You earn the opportunity based on who you were. But you will have the opportunity to thrive in it based on how you evolve. Remember, every day you are given a choice and a chance.

You get the choice to define how you want to lead inside this new context. You get the chance to dedicate time to consider the kind of person this role demands you become. That choice is about presence—choosing to slow down long enough to evaluate how you're showing up. The chance is about preparation—building new habits, asking better questions, seeking feedback before it's offered. Neither happens by default. You're going to need to set new goals. But more importantly, you'll need to hold space for unexpected realities. Circumstances will arise that challenge who you are and your beliefs. In those moments, interrupt circumstances with curiosity and positive intentions. Ask yourself: What is this moment trying to teach me? What does this tension reveal about what I still need to learn?

Plans change, but the goal stays the same. The early days of living in this move, won't follow your script. Obstacles will emerge. Timelines will shift. Resources may fall short. Push yourself to keep chasing that thing. Adaptability is your superpower, so flex it when needed and pivot when necessary. Stay the course. You will get to where you want to go; it might just take a little longer. Know that stuff happens, so be strong enough to push through it. The challenges that arise along the way are just a test of how badly you want it.

> Adaptability is your superpower, so flex it when needed and pivot when necessary.

In this chapter, you'll hear from four ambitious people who know exactly what it feels like to live in the move. Each person shares insights after living in the new move for only one or two years. They had to find their footing inside new roles that looked exciting from the outside but demanded deep internal recalibration once they stepped in.

These interviews offer insight into what it takes to thrive once you find yourself in that new opportunity you just took. You'll hear from Kenny Glenn, who stepped into a new entrepreneurial role and had to find confidence through early contributions. You'll hear from Kristen Brooks, who built and transitioned into a new career in consulting. You'll hear from Kristine Gilmore, who moved from leading others to developing leaders. And you'll hear from Antonio Shelton, a systems leader who was part of a team charged with collectively driving ambitious and strategic change These are real accounts of transition, resilience, and leadership in motion. Each voice offers a different lens into what it means to live in the move—to move with ambition, evolve with intention, and stay grounded in the face of change.

Interview: Kenny Glenn–"Remain Courageous"

Kenneth Glenn had been preparing for the moment long before the invitation arrived. As a motivational speaker, he now steps into rooms with confidence, passion, and a deep sense of purpose.

He built his voice through lived experience, shaped his message through reflection, and now uses both to reach others. His decision to commit fully to this lane came with pressure, but also peace. He knows where he's going, and he knows what he brings.

This section offers a window into the thoughts and habits that keep him moving forward. Kenny shares what grounds him as he grows into a new version of himself. These insights reflect the voice of someone who holds himself to a high standard and still makes space for learning along the way.

Insights

- **Build Real Relationships**: Kenny makes time for people. Whether through conversations at events or check-ins with trusted mentors, he stays open to learning through connection. Listening helps him grow. Being around people who stretch his thinking gives him ideas worth acting on.
- **Do More of What Works**: Kenny names the things that helped him succeed. He stays aware of the effort, attitude, and focus that helped him reach this moment. When he feels unsure, he goes back to the same qualities that shaped his earlier successes. They still hold value, so he keeps them close.
- **Choose Confidence Daily**: Kenny carries confidence as a decision. He believes in the work he's doing and the person he's becoming. That belief feels stronger now that he's living inside the move. He speaks with clarity, walks with purpose, and doesn't waste time questioning what he already knows to be true. He protects his confidence.
- **Follow Through With the Plan**: Kenny creates structure and holds himself to it. He places a high value on being prepared. His execution has focus. When he commits to take action, he carries it out. His consistency creates movement, and that

movement builds belief in what's possible in what's next for him.
- **Keep Showing Up with Purpose**: Kenny keeps going, even when he is still tackling something difficult. He holds on to the deeper reason behind his work. He does not back down from the challenge. He stays anchored in why he started, and that anchor helps him keep moving.

What struck me most in this conversation with Kenny Glenn was the way he commits to his decision. He made the move and he's living in it fully. His strength comes from the belief that he belongs here—and he proves it through conviction, self-trust, and an unwavering drive to give his best. He remains courageous by leading from who he is, not who others expect him to be.

Interview: Kristen Brooks–"Who I'm Becoming"

Kristen Brooks spent thirty years in education, committed to making a difference in her district. She launched tech labs, pushed for innovation, and showed up with consistent care for her students. Her drive came from a phrase she carried like a compass: "Mind the Gap." That was her commitment—to step in where something was missing and build solutions that served kids. That realization prompted a decision that would reshape her professional identity. Kristen stepped away from her district role to become an entrepreneur. She had a purpose and a willingness to figure it out.

Kristen shares what she has learned through the decision to step away from a long-held role and begin shaping a new one. It captures the uncertainty she faced, the values she carried forward, and the steady clarity that emerged as she built something of her own. These insights are reflections from someone who chose to keep growing. Each one invites you to think about your own journey, and what it might take to keep becoming who you're meant to be.

Insights

- **Remind Yourself Who You Want to Become:** "I was loyal to my district for thirty years." Kristen made a move that asked her to leave behind something familiar and step into something undefined. When things felt uncertain, she found clarity by returning to the question: Who do I want to become? That reflection helped her steady her thinking and keep moving forward with intention.

- **Place Value on Your Voice and What It Can Offer:** "My voice is important—I live and believe that voice is important." Kristen gave herself permission to speak from experience and act on what she knew to be true. She saw a need in education and stepped in with solutions. Her voice became something she now allows others to see and hear more fully.

- **Confidence Comes From What You've Already Done:** "I've relied on previous experiences and successes to work through this." Starting over brought moments that tested Kristen's belief in herself. She didn't pretend to have all the answers. When she felt uncertain, she looked back at what she had already achieved and used that lived experience to inspire her next move.

- **Don't Let Your Negative Self Overtake Your Positive One:** "Never let your negative thoughts overtake your positive self." Kristen named what many experience but rarely say out loud. On hard days, self-doubt made her question if she was doing enough or moving fast enough. In those moments, she reminded herself that one discouraging thought doesn't deserve full control. She focused on staying rooted in her joy and belief.

- **If Purpose Aligns, Give Yourself Permission to Explore:** "If purpose aligns, I give myself permission to explore the partnership." Every decision in Kristen's new role came back to one filter: Does this align with what I believe kids need? That sense of purpose became a guide. It gave her clarity when opportunities surfaced and helped her decide where to invest her energy and where to hold it back.

What struck me most in this conversation with Kristen Brooks was how identity surfaced as something you continue shaping with every new decision. Kristen's journey showed me that becoming a new version of yourself is a process of remembering what is important to you, even while discovering who you're still learning to be.

Interview: Kristine Gilmore–"Living In Purpose-Driven Work"

Kristine Gilmore served as a superintendent for nearly two decades. Her work was defined by care, leadership, and a deep commitment to the community she led. When she chose to transition out of the role, it wasn't because she had reached a ceiling. It was because she had reached a place of being ready to explore a new passion for purpose-driven work. She saw an opportunity to contribute in a new way—by building up other leaders and helping them extend their reach.

This section captures the mindset and intentional habits that helped Kristine carry her ambition into a new space. Her insights offer a calm, grounded reflection on what it means to continue growing when the title changes but the mission stays clear.

Insights

- **Your Confidence Grows With Each New Stretch:** "New role, new experience. It will be harder at first." Kristine didn't expect instant comfort in the new role. She gave herself time to settle in. Her confidence grew through the process of showing up, learning new approaches, and trusting that her skill set would transfer. Each stretch became another step toward being more comfortable in the new role.

- **Adults Can Take Risks, Too:** "We ask kids to take risks every day. Adults can, too." Kristine saw risk-taking as a professional responsibility. She understood that stepping into unfamiliar spaces wasn't a sign of weakness. It was a sign of growth. Her willingness to embrace discomfort created new space for learning and leadership.
- **Do the Self-Work Before the Role Changes:** "Sometimes the opportunity shows up before you think you're ready." Kristine spoke about the internal preparation she undertook before making the move. She took the time to ask herself what mattered, how she wanted to show up, and what kind of leadership felt most aligned with her values. That work made the transition more intentional.
- **Finding Fulfillment in a Reimagined Impact:** "I'm OK being the supporting cast now." Kristine didn't need to be the final decision-maker to feel purposeful. She found meaning in equipping others and helping them lead well. Her satisfaction came from knowing her efforts built something that would continue through others.
- **Remained Grounded in Purpose-Driven Work:** "My values aligned with the mission. That's why I said yes to this opportunity." She carried her sense of purpose—she brought it into her new context. The alignment between her beliefs and the organization's mission gave her clarity. That clarity anchored her through the change and reminded her why she took advantage of this opportunity.

What struck me most in this conversation with Kristine Gilmore was how clearly she carried her purpose into a new context. Her decision to move was about choosing where she could serve best.

Watching her lead without needing the spotlight reminded me that leadership doesn't disappear when the role changes. It just takes a new shape.

Interview: Antonio Shelton–"A Unified Team Living the Move"

Superintendent Antonio Shelton stepped into his role at Santa Monica-Malibu Unified School District with a clear priority: bring a team together around a shared ambition. He focused on building something sustainable. From the beginning, he made it a habit to ask himself and others if they were truly prepared for the leadership the work required.

The Executive Team that joined him supported a district with history, with progress already in motion, and with a need for deeper alignment. Together, they decided to set direction through collaboration, define clear priorities, and develop habits that would help them lead with purpose. Their work reflects what it looks like when a team makes a move and lives that move with consistency.

This interview with Superintendent Shelton offers a window into how a unified team approaches leadership when the goal is to shape it. It surfaces the daily habits, decisions, and moments of unity that helped this team make forward progress while holding on to their shared values. It shows what becomes possible when a team agrees to move together.

Insights

- **Alignment is a Team Decision:** "Are you surrounded by individuals who will support you?" That's the first question Shelton asked when preparing for the work ahead. He treated getting aligned as a shared commitment that had to be acted upon regularly. The team built trust by being honest with each other, remaining clear about what they wanted to achieve, and making sure everyone understood how their role connected to the whole. Becoming aligned as a team was part of how they operated every day.

- **Shared Strategy, Shared Stakes:** "I value collaboration. We co-developed the plan and that gave people ownership." The pillars in the strategic plan were built by the team. Each leader had space to name what they saw, what they believed was possible, and what needed to change. That kind of contribution created deep investment. When the team saw their thinking reflected in the work, they took greater responsibility for moving it forward.
- **Welcome Course Correction:** "The team welcomes course correction. That mindset helps us move forward." The feedback process was built into how they operated. Shelton and his team treated reflection as part of the structure. When something didn't land well, or when conditions shifted, they were quick to collect feedback from others. Feedback created better strategic decision making and gave space for them to adjust plans. Their approach helped them respond faster and stay focused on results.
- **Keep Recalibrating:** "I had to make sure people were committed to not being disjointed." There were moments when things fell out of sync. Relationships changed. Unexpected challenges surfaced. In those moments, Shelton paid close attention and revisited expectations, clarified responsibilities, and returned to the habits that grounded their work. That practice helped the team stay calibrated in moments of uncertainty.
- **Showcase the Work in Progress:** "Put your work on display as you cultivate it." The team made intentional choices to share the work as it was happening. They invited others to see the process, understand the thinking, and connect to the purpose.

That openness helped build trust. It also gave others a reason to care about the outcome. Showing the work made it easier to bring people along and helped the team build momentum.

What struck me most in this conversation with Superintendent Shelton was how a team deciding to move together on purpose was a choice—and that choice, made repeatedly, is what strengthened their connection and unity as a team.

You've now heard from four ambitious individuals who made their move. Each person stepped into something they once only imagined and shared what it really feels like to live on the other side of that decision. Their reflections offer a closer look at the mindset, habits, and choices that helped them thrive as they transitioned into their new context. These insights are here to center you as you prepare for your own transition:

1. **Remain Courageous** Kenny Glenn reminded us what it looks like to live inside a decision you fully believe in. The move was his, and he carried it with a confidence that grew stronger the deeper he went. You don't need to prove anything to anyone. Just keep proving to yourself that you're still all in.
2. **Do the Self-Work in Advance** Kristine Gilmore showed us the power of preparation that starts before the opportunity arrives. She did the internal work early—clarifying who she was, what she valued, and how she wanted to grow. That kind of self-work gives you something to return to when you need it. The more you know yourself, the better you'll move through what's next.
3. **Calibrate Often, and Trust the Team to Grow Into the Work** Antonio Shelton helped us see what it looks like when a team moves together with purpose. The team stayed

aligned by talking honestly, adjusting when needed, and holding each other to a shared standard. If you keep tuning in and building together, you'll grow into the work you set out to do.

4. **Keep Showing Up–Impact Grows Over Time** Each person we interviewed encountered moments of uncertainty. Some faced slow starts. Others questioned if they were ready. But they kept showing up. You can celebrate the progress you are making by focusing on tackling the new momentum markers you set as you transition into your new context.

5. **Invest in a Support System That Invests In You** The people we spoke to all pointed to the importance of relationships. Mentors. Collaborators. Friends who speak truth and encouragement. A strong support system is necessary. Choose people who remind you who you are and push you to keep becoming who you're meant to be. Engage your trusted network.

6. **Honor the Decision. Keep Becoming the Person Who Made It** Every move you make starts with a choice. And every choice reflects something you believe about yourself. The version of you that stepped into this transition had a reason. Keep becoming that person. Let the decision grow you, not weigh on you.

7. **Let Yourself Be a Beginner Again** Kristine said it best: "We ask kids to take risks every day. Adults can take a risk too." Stepping into something new means being willing to learn again, stretch again, ask questions again. You don't need to act like you know everything. You just need to stay open enough to grow.

Reflection: Living in the Move

Each story shared in this chapter was rooted in lived experience. They were layered, personal, and often uncomfortable. The people you heard from were real about their doubts, intentional with their choices, and honest about what it took to move forward. They showed us that making a move is about becoming someone new.

Take a moment now to revisit the insights and lessons from this chapter. Let them settle in. Name what connected with you. Name what stirred something real. The goal is not to mimic anyone else's path—it's to build the awareness of who you need and want to become when you find yourself living in your own move.

Reflection Activity: Who Are You Becoming?

Set aside ten minutes. Find a quiet space. Be real with yourself as you answer the questions below:

1. **What did you see in these stories that reminded you of yourself right now?** Let this question pull you into the reality of your own transition. What resonated? What stirred something in you that you didn't expect?
2. **Who do you want to become in your next chapter?** Give yourself permission to name the person you are becoming—not just the title or the role, but the version of you that this move is asking for.
3. **What daily mindset or habit will keep you grounded as you grow into this version of yourself?** Name one thing. What will help you return to your center when things feel uncertain?

For free *Make Your Move* resources visit: www.marlonstyles/resources

CONCLUSION

Make Your Move

To *Move with Ambition* is to find strength in the inspiration that lives in your heart, act decisively on what matters most, and stay deeply connected to your highest aspirations. At the start of this book, I introduced you to a young man named Tanner—a former student of mine back when I was on *Team Ambition* at Pleasant Run Middle School. I shared that story for one reason: to honor the relationship that made me fall in love with being in education. By name, Tanner is the student who helped me find purpose. I thought I was pouring everything I had into him, trying to be a positive influence, trying to give him all I could. What I didn't realize at the time was that he was having a life-changing impact on me. For the first time in my professional journey, I could say with certainty that I loved what I was doing. It wasn't a moment of recognition or some external validation that brought that clarity, it was a relationship. It was a student. It was a young man named Tanner who lit something in me I didn't know was missing.

I bring him back into this conversation now to remind you of something that matters: that feeling—the feeling of love for the work you do—is worth holding on to. And even more than that, it's worth returning to when you find yourself uncertain, tired, or pulled away from the reasons that brought you here in the first place. So I'll ask you again: Who or what made you fall in love with what you do? Or, if you're still discovering your path—who or what made you fall in love with what you want to do?

This is more than a reflective prompt. It's a critical part of your ambitious identity. When you stay close to what you love, you unlock a greater sense of what's possible. That connection strengthens your belief and helps you recognize opportunity when it arrives. I've stayed grounded in what makes me love this work. Move after move, role after role, I return to the feeling that Tanner gave me. That feeling reminds me that something meaningful could be around the corner. It gives me the energy to keep moving forward, open to what's next.

My challenge for you is to name what brings you that same joy. Name what reminds you that your ambitions are worth pursuing. Stay so connected to it that it shapes how you think, how you lead, and how you make decisions. Before you name your next ambition or take your next step, name the source of your love. Hold onto the person or the experience that taught you why this matters. Let that memory serve as your source of truth.

There are moments when the right words find you at the right time. There's another person I want to bring back into focus before we close—someone who shaped the core of this book in a different way. You may remember Mr. Farmer. I call him Coach. You met him back in the Introduction. One day, during a conversation that shaped my entire professional outlook, I asked him a question I had been carrying for a long time. I wanted to know how you could tell when you're ready to step into a bigger opportunity.

Mr. Farmer had a way of saying things that made you stop and think. He was the one who looked me in the eye during a private meeting and gave me this piece of advice: "You will never be ready, but you *can* begin preparing for the big move."

Every time I found myself standing at the edge of something new, I could hear his voice. "Prepare. Learn." That message stayed with me. Over time, it became one of the most important truths I carry with me as a leader and a person. The idea that preparation is always within your control. That's the same invitation I've extended to you across every chapter of this book.

You've done a lot through these chapters. You've reflected on your habits. You've aligned with your purpose. You've shaped a belief system that can carry you when things get hard. You've done the real work of naming the ambitious move you want to make—not a title, not a role, but a meaningful shift toward the future you're trying to build. You've created space for new behaviors and positioned yourself for this moment.

Now it comes down to something very real. Will you dedicate yourself to the daily discipline of staying prepared? Preparation isn't a one-time effort. It's a mindset. It's a decision you renew each day. It's what allows you to build momentum, stay grounded, and step forward with confidence when the opportunity appears.

> Preparation isn't a one-time effort. It's a mindset. It's a decision you renew each day. It's what allows you to build momentum, stay grounded, and step forward with confidence when the opportunity appears.

You've seen examples. Neil Gupta's story showed you the years of behind-the-scenes preparation he put in before stepping into the superintendency. Kristine Gilmore showed you how inner work and self-awareness strengthened her readiness to walk into something new. They didn't arrive at readiness by accident. They made decisions long before the opportunity came.

You are now in that same position. The move ahead of you will be shaped by what you choose to own, what you choose to allow, and what you're willing to change.

There's a point in every journey when it becomes clear that you're standing at an intersection. It doesn't always look dramatic from the outside. But inside, it feels weighty. Important. Defining. In my experience, that moment always starts with a question:

How brave do I want to be?

I believe there are two kinds of people who show up at this moment when they must decide if they are going to make their move. Both are fully capable. Both have a story. Both have desire. And both are having an internal conversation right now.

The first person or team sits with their thoughts longer than they expected to. This person or team is full of ambition, they have their eye on an ambitious move, but for some reason they are hesitant to go for it or still struggle with making the commitment to themselves to act on it. They have a deep desire to make that ambitious move, but they are unsure if desire is enough.

The internal conversation might include a series of questions they ask themselves:

- What if I'm not as ready as I thought I was?
- What if people are expecting more from me than I can give right now?
- What if this new role exposes everything I'm still trying to figure out?
- What if I disappoint the people who believe in me?

- What if I waited until next year to think about doing this?
- Should I wait until I feel more confident?
- What if I'm just now what they are looking for and pick somebody else?
- Would it be better to keep doing what I'm doing right now?
- What happens if I make this move and I fail?

Hard questions are being asked because this person wants their next move to reflect the care they put into their work. This kind of internal dialogue deserves time, space, and some attention. If this is the conversation you're sitting in, give yourself room to process what's taking shape. Schedule time with someone you trust. Talk through what you're carrying. Say the questions out loud. Sometimes gaining clarity begins by speaking the things you haven't had the chance to say. A mentor, colleague, or close peer can help you hear your own thinking more clearly. It's worth being walked through with someone who wants to see you be successful. As someone who has wrestled with this kind of internal dialogue, I invite you to list the conditions that would make you feel supported in taking this next step. Then explore how to start building those conditions. Consider making one small move this week that helps you test or explore the direction you're considering. Create space for your takeaways to inform your decision making. Lastly, get yourself focused and get a gameplan that will build the confidence you need to make your move.

This second person or team is absolutely ready. They have momentum on their side and welcome what's next with full commitment. The opportunity ahead lights something up inside of them. Every part of them is leaning forward. Their internal dialogue is fueled by belief in themselves and a trust in everything they have done to prepare themselves for this opportunity. They're imagining the first big move they'll make when they step into the opportunity.

The internal conversation might include a series of commitments they use to encourage themselves:

- I'm going to show up and give it everything I've got.
- I've put in the work to be here.
- This feels right.
- I've been building toward this, even if I didn't realize it at first.
- I know what I'm capable of, and I'm ready to show it.
- This is the right time for me to take the next step.
- I've earned the chance to walk into this with confidence.
- Whatever comes my way, I know I will figure it out.
- I've done enough preparation—it's time to move.
- I believe in myself and what I bring to the table.
- I'm excited to see what's possible.

There's no second-guessing here, just a sense of confidence to go for it. This person or team knows what this moment represents, and they know what it took to reach this point. The internal conversation feels more like a period of affirmation and celebration. If this is where you are, stay locked in. Keep listening to the voice that brought you this far. Trust your preparation. Make a move that honors the work you've done to get to this point.

These two conversations reveal something meaningful, both are signs that the person is thinking deeply about what matters and cares about getting this next step right. One person is still sorting through the pressure of the decision, and the other is stepping into it with full confidence. There's nothing easy about deciding to make your move, but there's something powerful about recognizing when the moment asks more of you. The question: *How brave do I want to be?* is worth sitting with. Let it guide how you might be processing the decision. And if that question stays with you long enough, it eventually leads to another one that deserves your full attention: *How bad do I want it?* All I ask is that your answers to these two questions come from a place of belief and not ego. I ask that they come from a place of honesty with yourself.

I believe you will.

Because you're not the same person who started this book. You've taken ownership of your habits. You've asked harder questions of yourself. You've stopped waiting for someone else to decide when it's your time. You've learned how to build movement by aligning your ambition with your purpose.

Whatever version of you that is showing up right now, you get to carry it forward.

When you find yourself second-guessing, come back to this truth: You don't prepare for the opportunity you have. You prepare for the opportunity you want.

Let that guide you.

Before we close, I want to say something directly to you. Just me talking to you, the person who made the choice to take this journey seriously.

I'm proud of you.

Not because you finished the book. Because of the way you showed up inside it. You've made space for hard reflections. You've let yourself grow. You've chosen to think deeply about your purpose and your path. That takes courage.

> You don't prepare for the opportunity you have. You prepare for the opportunity you want.

You've made decisions that no one else can see, and that matters, too. You've kept showing up, while still chasing that opportunity. That's strength. You've carried the weight of expectation while still trying to stay true to your own beliefs. That's leadership. I want you to know—I see that effort. And I believe in where it will take you. You don't need permission from anyone but yourself to take your next step. You've already earned it. So here's what I'll leave you with:

> Keep preparing.
> Keep showing up.
> Keep becoming.
> You are ready.
> You are capable.
> And you are the one who gets to decide what happens next.

I'll be watching quietly, expectantly, and with full belief in what's ahead for you.

Your moment will come. And when it does...

Make Your Move.

Visit **marlonstyles.com/resources**
for free *Make Your Move* resources, study questions, and tools.

References

Brooks, K. (2025, February 14). *Personal interview.*

Clear, J. (2018). *Atomic habits: An easy & proven way to build good habits & break bad ones.* Avery.

Covey, S. R. (1989). *The 7 habits of highly effective people: Powerful lessons in personal change.* Free Press.

Duhigg, C. (2012). *The power of habit: Why we do what we do in life and business.* Random House.

Dweck, C. S. (2006). *Mindset: The new psychology of success.* Random House.

Ganz, M. (2011). *Public narrative, collective action, and power.* In S. Odugbemi & T. Lee (Eds.), Accountability through public opinion: From inertia to public action (pp. 273–289). Washington, DC: World Bank

Gilmore, C. (2025, February 20). *Personal interview.*

Glenn, K. (2025, February 12). *Personal interview.*

Keller, G., & Papasan, J. (2013). *The one thing: The surprisingly simple truth behind extraordinary results.* Bard Press.

Locke, E. A., & Latham, G. P. (2002). Building a practically useful theory of goal setting and task motivation: A 35-year odyssey. *American Psychologist, 57*(9), 705–717.

Shelton, A. (2025, February 7). *Personal interview.*

Sinek, S. (2009). *Start with why: How great leaders inspire everyone to take action.* Portfolio.

Acknowledgements

Thank you to Kenny Glenn, Kristen Brooks, Kristine Gilmore, Neil Gupta, and Antonio Shelton for sharing your stories and lending your voices to this work. I'm grateful to my colleagues and teammates over the years for trusting me to serve alongside you and for the shared commitment to meaningful, ambitious work. A special thank you to Tanner Lowe and Mark Farmer for the lasting impact you've had on my life. And to my friends and family, your support means everything.

About the Author

Marlon Styles is a recognized inspirational speaker and educational leader. In 2017, he was named a Top 30 Digital Trailblazer by the Center for Digital Education. Under his leadership at Middletown City Schools, the district was awarded the ISTE Distinguished District Award in 2019. He testified before the United States Congress in 2020 to advocate for access and opportunity for all students. K-12 Dive recognized him as the Superintendent of the Year in 2020 for his advocacy and leadership on a national stage. In 2025, he was named one of the Top 100 Education Influencers by District Administration. Styles' mission is to inspire educators to see themselves as empowered *Unifiers* capable of creating the types of learning experiences today's modern learners need to thrive.

As a superintendent and keynote speaker, Styles has earned national recognition for his impact, including the ISTE Distinguished District Award, being named Superintendent of the Year by K–12 Dive, and recognized as one of the Top 100 Education Influencers by District Administration.

What brings him the most joy is helping others believe in what's possible. He leads with purpose, stays curious about what's possible, and believes deeply in the power of people. Whether coaching teams, speaking on stage, or designing leadership strategies, Styles sees every moment as an opportunity to connect, inspire, and move with intention. He shows up as an *Igniter of energy*, a *Reformer of systems*, and a *Unifier of people and purpose*. He continues to build spaces in which individuals and teams can lead boldly, grow intentionally, and do the work that truly matters. **Connect with Marlon:**

- Website: marlonstyles.com
- Facebook: MarlonStylesJr
- Instagram: Marlon_StylesJr
- LinkedIn: MarlonStylesJr
- X: Styles_MarlonJr

More from ConnectEDD Publishing

Since 2015, ConnectEDD has worked to transform education by empowering educators to become better-equipped to teach, learn, and lead. What started as a small company designed to provide professional learning events for educators has grown to include a variety of services to help educators and administrators address essential challenges. ConnectEDD offers instructional and leadership coaching, professional development workshops focusing on a variety of educational topics, a roster of nationally recognized educator associates who possess hands-on knowledge and experience, educational conferences custom-designed to meet the specific needs of schools, districts, and state/national organizations, and ongoing, personalized support, both virtually and onsite. In 2020, ConnectEDD expanded to include publishing services designed to provide busy educators with books and resources consisting of practical information on a wide variety of teaching, learning, and leadership topics. Please visit us online at connecteddpublishing.com or contact us at: info@connecteddpublishing.com

Recent Publications:

Live Your Excellence: Action Guide by Jimmy Casas

Culturize: Action Guide by Jimmy Casas

Daily Inspiration for Educators: Positive Thoughts for Every Day of the Year by Jimmy Casas

Eyes on Culture: Multiply Excellence in Your School by Emily Paschall

Pause. Breathe. Flourish. Living Your Best Life as an Educator by William D. Parker

L.E.A.R.N.E.R. Finding the True, Good, and Beautiful in Education by Marita Diffenbaugh

Educator Reflection Tips Volume II: Refining Our Practice by Jami Fowler-White

Handle With Care: Managing Difficult Situations in Schools with Dignity and Respect by Jimmy Casas and Joy Kelly

Disruptive Thinking: Preparing Learners for Their Future by Eric Sheninger

Permission to be Great: Increasing Engagement in Your School by Dan Butler

Daily Inspiration for Educators: Positive Thoughts for Every Day of the Year, Volume II by Jimmy Casas

The 6 Literacy Levers: Creating a Community of Readers by Brad Gustafson

The Educator's ATLAS: Your Roadmap to Engagement by Weston Kieschnick

In This Season: Words for the Heart by Todd Nesloney, LaNesha Tabb, Tanner Olson, and Alice Lee

MORE FROM CONNECTEDD PUBLISHING

Leading with a Humble Heart: A 40-Day Devotional for Leaders by Zac Bauermaster

Recalibrate the Culture: Our Why...Our Work...Our Values by Jimmy Casas

Creating Curious Classrooms: The Beauty of Questions by Emma Chiappetta

Crafting the Culture: 45 Reflections on What Matters Most by Joe Sanfelippo and Jeffrey Zoul

Improving School Mental Health: The Thriving School Community Solution by Charle Peck and Dr. Cameron Caswell

Building Authenticity: A Blueprint for the Leader Inside You by Todd Nesloney and Tyler Cook

Connecting Through Conversation: A Playbook for Talking with Kids by Erika Bare and Tiffany Burns

The Dream Factory: Designing a Purposeful Life by Mark Trumbo

Stories Behind Stances: Creating Empathy Through Hearing "The Other Side" by Chris Singleton

Happy Eyes: Becoming All Things to All People by Ryan Tillman

The Generative Age: Artificial Intelligence and the Future of Education by Alana Winnick

Recalibrate the Culture: Action Guide by Jimmy Casas

Leading with PEOPLE: A Six Pillar Framework for Fruitful Leadership by Zac Bauermaster

A School Leader's Guide to Reclaiming Purpose by Frederick C. Buskey

Foundations of an Elite Culture: Building Success with High Standards and a Positive Environment by David Arencibia

Personalize: Meeting the Needs of All Learners by Eric Sheninger and Nicki Slaugh

The Five Principles of Educator Professionalism: Rebuilding Trust in Schools by Nason Lollar

Words on the Wall: Culturizing Your Classroom For Observable Impact by Jimmy Casas and Cale Birk

School of Engagement: 45 Activities to Ignite Student Learning by Jonathan Alsheimer

Intentional Instructional Moves: Strategic Steps to Accelerate Student Learning by Sherry St. Clair

Overcoming Education: Complex Challenges, Difficult People, and the Art of Making a Difference by Brad R. Gustafson

The Language of Behavior: A Framework to Elevate Student Success by Charle Peck and Joshua Stamper

Whose Permission Are You Waiting For? An Educator's Guide to Doing What You Love by William D. Parker

The Leader You're Not…And Why It's Just As Important As the Leader You Are by Scott Borba

The Growth-Minded Leader by Tyler Cook

Day by Day: 180 Days of Hope and Encouragement by Zac Bauermaster

www.ingramcontent.com/pod-product-compliance
Lightning Source LLC
Chambersburg PA
CBHW070625030426
42337CB00020B/3915